SCHOLASTIC

Teaching With Favorite READ-ALOUDS in PreK

50 Must-Have Books with Lessons and Activities That Build Skills in Vocabulary, Comprehension, and More

By Susan Lunsford

New York • Toronto • London • Auckland • Sydney
Mexico City • New Delhi • Hong Kong • Buenos Aires

Teaching Resources

DEDICATION

"Reading to your little ones is just like
putting gold coins in the bank.
It will pay you back tenfold . . ."

— From *Read to Your Bunny* by Rosemary Wells, page 25

For Ryan & Maddie
My little ones

For Brad:
For adding gold coins to our little ones' bank with books at bedtime

For Miss Christy and the children of Fairbrook First Steps Preschool

For Joanna and Sarah:
Thanks for your guidance and support.

Scholastic Inc. grants teachers permission to photocopy the reproducibles from this book for classroom use. No other part of this publication may be reproduced in whole or in part, or stored in a retrieval system, or transmitted in any form or by any means, electronic, mechanical, photocopying, recording, or otherwise, without permission of the publisher. For information regarding permission, write to Scholastic Professional Books, 524 Broadway, New York, NY 10012-3999.

Cover design by Josuè Castilleja
Cover photograph by James Levin
Interior Design by LDL Designs, based on a design by Sarah Morrow
Interior illustrations by Sharon Holm

Copyright © 2004 by Susan Lunsford. All rights reserved.

ISBN 0-439-40416-9

Printed in the U.S.A.

2 3 4 5 6 7 8 9 10 40 10 09 08 07 06 05 04

CONTENTS

First Steps: I Love That Book! Read It Again!

My own test-kids: Ryan and Maddie "reading" favorite books

"Where are the kids?" my husband asked one evening when he wasn't greeted by the usual stampede to the front door by our four- and six-year-old children chanting, "Daddy's home, Daddy's home, Daddy's home!"

"You're right," I admitted. "It's too quiet, isn't it?" Together we walked back to the hall and stopped outside of Maddie's room. There, in the middle of a heap of every book the two of them own (which is many, I assure you), were our children, perfectly engrossed in the books.

"Daddy's home," Maddie commented, although rather absent-mindedly. She immediately returned to the pictures in Bruce Degan's *Jamberry*. "Guess what, Daddy? I've already picked out our books for bedtime tonight. Look! I found *How Do Dinosaurs Say Goodnight?*"

My husband loosened his tie, gave me a look, and said, "We'll be sure to dig the two of you out of that pile of books in time for bed."

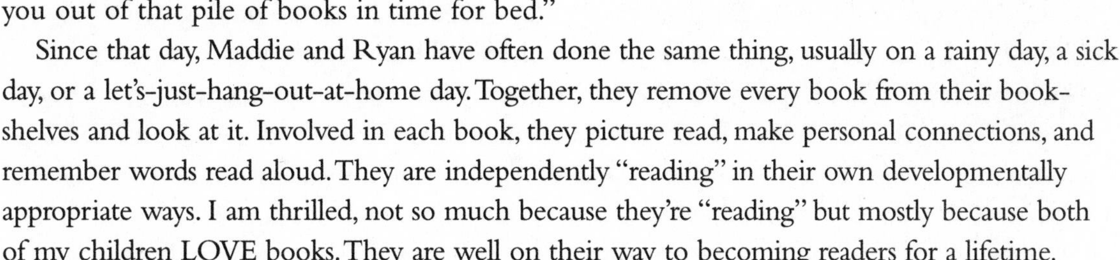

Since that day, Maddie and Ryan have often done the same thing, usually on a rainy day, a sick day, or a let's-just-hang-out-at-home day. Together, they remove every book from their bookshelves and look at it. Involved in each book, they picture read, make personal connections, and remember words read aloud. They are independently "reading" in their own developmentally appropriate ways. I am thrilled, not so much because they're "reading" but mostly because both of my children LOVE books. They are well on their way to becoming readers for a lifetime.

Ryan and Maddie's love of books was inevitable. They've been surrounded by quality works of literature since infancy. There are books in every room of our house—cookbooks in the kitchen, books in progress on our night stands, baskets and shelves of books and magazines in every bedroom, bathroom, and on every coffee table, and books on tape in our cars. We go to the library every other week and attend story hour at our local bookstore. Books at bedtime are never skipped. Books are a part of our daily lives. And my enthusiasm for the books shared with them is genuine.

As a teacher for twelve years and a mother of two small children, I've written this book from the overlapping perspectives of teacher and mother. Throughout the book, I have used my very own test-kids, Ryan and Maddie, and the children of Fairbrook First Steps Preschool (my children's preschool) to decide which books are must-reads for preschoolers. Their preference for particular books has reinforced my belief that some books are better at instilling a love of reading than others. So the question for the teachers and the parents of preschoolers is not how important it is to read to children, the question is *what* to read.

The cheers when a favorite books is displayed, the pleas to "read it again," and the contagious belly laughs as I've read the escapades featuring these favorite book characters prove that some books are better at motivating prereaders to learn to read. Since motivation is the very first step necessary to enter the world of reading, it is important that the first books shared in these formative years make a lasting impression.

A Preschool Child Taking First Steps to Reading Will:

1. identify favorite books
2. look at books as a self-selected activity
3. ask questions and initiate talk about books
4. look forward to anticipated time for read-aloud in his or her daily routine
5. be engaged in the book being shared—showing pleasure, surprise, sadness, happiness with regard to characters and plot

The following 50 great books should be a part of every preschooler's read-aloud experience. After reading these books for pure enjoyment, strengthen prereading strategies, enhance vocabulary, and meet learning objectives across the curriculum with the fun book-related activities that accommodate all learning levels.

A Few Words About the Read-Aloud and Rich Vocabulary Connection

It's no surprise that by their senior year, students at the top of their class know about four times as many words as their lower performing classmates. "Most chilling, however," write Beck, McKeown, and Kucan in *Bringing Words to Life* (pages 1–2), "is the finding that once established, such differences appear difficult to ameliorate. This is clearly very bad news!"

The good news is that implementing effective vocabulary instruction has become a priority in elementary schools. Techniques for providing the most effective and meaningful vocabulary instruction have also been identified. For preschool teachers, the most appropriate place to begin is with a daily read-aloud, which gives the opportunity to teach one or two new words. Read-aloud time will provide a wealth of vocabulary words in meaningful contexts over the course of the school year.

In the pages of my book, I highlight one or more words from each of the 50 must-have read-aloud books. Activities and direct examples from my classroom illustrate how to best present words from trade books to help preschoolers commit new word knowledge to memory and to apply these newly discovered words in new situations.

When sharing a wordless picture book, look for a prevailing theme or level-appropriate word to highlight for vocabulary instruction. In *1,2,3 to the Zoo*, for example, the animals board a train. The word *aboard* is introduced as a rich vocabulary word for describing the characters' actions. The word and definition are reinforced in future retellings of the story.

Chapter 1: Meet Mother Goose and Friends

10 Must-Have Books of Read-Aloud Rhymes

Chapter Learning Goals:

- enhancing reading with fluency and expression
- developing phonemic awareness
- understanding that print conveys meaning and is organized
- using beginning letter clues
- using context clues
- exploring the beat of rhyming texts
- strengthening oral language skills
- exploring rhyming words in the context of rhyming books

There is no better way to get preschoolers to love books than to use the excessive energy they are so full of to stomp and romp and clap and chant to the beat of great read-aloud rhymes. Read-aloud rhymes provide young children with opportunities to do the following:

- answer comprehension questions
- explore rhyming and nonsense words
- feel the beat and rhythm of language
- extend vocabulary
- stimulate discussion
- inspire creative writing ideas
- memorize short rhymes
- use context clues to sound out words
- develop phonemic awareness
- participate in choral rereadings

Read *My Very First Mother Goose, Here Comes Mother Goose*, and *Tomie dePaola's Mother Goose* to introduce young children to Frau Gosen (later known as Mother Goose) and continue her storytelling tradition to a new generation of young readers and rhymers. Share *Read-Aloud Rhymes for the Very Young,* and then discuss the kid-friendly poems. Enjoy the beat of *Wiggle Waggle Fun* during read-aloud time.

Make a list of the rhyming words in *Sheep in a Jeep*. Combine words and movement with your reading of *Tumble Bumble*. Let your preschoolers ponder the questions posed in the titles of *Mr. Brown Can Moo! Can You?* and *Is Your Mama a Llama?* Explore letters sounds with *Jamberry*.

10 Must-Have Books of Read-Aloud Rhymes

My Very First Mother Goose edited by Iona Opie

Here Comes Mother Goose edited by Iona Opie

Read-Aloud Rhymes for the Very Young selected by Jack Prelutsky

Wiggle Waggle Fun by Margaret Mayo

Tomie dePaola's Mother Goose by Tomie dePaola

Sheep in a Jeep by Nancy Shaw

Tumble Bumble by Felicia Bond

Mr. Brown Can Moo! Can You? by Dr. Seuss

Is Your Mama a Llama? by Deborah Guarino

Jamberry by Bruce Degan

My Very First Mother Goose

edited by Iona Opie

LEARNING ABOUT Reading Fluency

If there's one book that I feel every preschooler should have in his or her read-aloud repertoire, it's a collection of Mother Goose rhymes. This belief was reaffirmed a few years ago when I heard Rosemary Wells speak at a children's literature conference and refer to Mother Goose as "the Shakespeare of Preschool and Kindergarten." She went on to remind us teachers and librarians that "once something is lost from our culture, it cannot be replaced." I feel certain these two ideals were the driving force behind Iona Opie and Rosemary Wells' collaboration on *My Very First Mother Goose.*

Having fun with Mother Goose

Like Rosemary Wells, I believe every child should know about the old woman who lived in a shoe, the cow that jumped over the moon, and the three little kittens who lost their mittens. Mother Goose helps youngsters count, learn their alphabet, identify body parts, and pat-a-cake with the best of them.

In the mini-lesson that follows, enter Mother Goose's rhyming world to build reading fluency and to explore phonemic awareness and beginning letter clues—all in one read-aloud session that you can adapt to suit the needs of your class. Select rhymes to focus on one skill a day or a sampling

Rich Vocabulary

rapping *v.* making a noise by hitting something

of skills as I've done. However the lesson progresses, your preschoolers are sure to fall under Mother Goose's spell as you play with language during this read-along, read-aloud time.

Mrs. L.: Today we're going to play a game with Mother Goose to practice reading her rhymes aloud. I'll open the book to any page—

Zachary: I hope you open it to the pig in the car.

Victoria: I hope you open it to "Good Morning Mrs. Hen."

Mrs. L.: I'll give you all a chance to tell me your favorites, but first let's just open the book to—

Rachel: "The Brave Duke."

Mrs. L.: You're right. Look at the first letter of this poem for a hint about how this rhyme begins.

Blake: It starts with the letter *O*.

Ryan: That's not *Brave* because that starts with a *B*.

Ben: I think the word is *Oh*—like *Oh, my*.

Ryan: No the letter is *O*.

Mrs. L.: You're both right. The word is *Oh* and it starts with the letter *O*. Please be my echo as we read this rhyme. I'll whisper a line from the poem. You'll be my echo and repeat it after me. *(I whisper the following line.)* "Oh, the brave old duke of York."

Class: "Oh, the brave old duke of York." *(We continue reading the poem using the whisper-and-echo strategy.)*

Mrs. L.: Great! Let's read it again. This time, clap along. *(We repeat the rhyme, clapping to the beat.)* What great rhythm! Let's open the book to another page—

Megan: It's the black hen one!

Blake: It can't start with *Black Hen*. It must be Hen because of the big letter *H*.

Mrs. L.: Let's look at the first word: *H-I-C-K-E-T-Y*. What hints do these letters give you?

Jared: It starts with *H*, but it can't be *Hen* because there's no *n*.

Mrs. L.: Good thinking. What letter sounds does this word have?

Tommy: *C-K*.

Brittany: And *T*. It's *Hickety*.

Rachel: Yes! "Hickety pickety my black hen!"

Mrs. L.: Great job of using the letter clues.

Rachel: I used my brain—I remembered the *pickety* word was next. The picture of the black hen helped, too.

TEACHING TIP

To get prereaders reciting rhymes as a class, use a whisper-and-echo strategy. Whisper a line to the class ("Baa baa black sheep have you any wool?"), and then invite children to be your echo and repeat the line.

Chunk the words together into lengths your class can echo ("Baa baa black sheep/have you any wool?/Yes, sir, yes, sir,/three bags full.") Because the whisper-and-echo strategy promotes greater participation, it is an effective way to stimulate oral language development and to reinforce reading with fluency and expression.

Mrs. L.: Excellent! Please be my echo as I read the lines in this rhyme. *(We read the poem using the whisper-and-echo strategy. Then we repeat the rhyme, this time tapping to the beat.)* Nice job. Let's try another rhyme. Megan, would you please choose a poem for us to share?

Megan: "Star light, Star bright,"—it's my favorite! I always say this one when I see my first star at night.

Casey: Does your wish come true?

Megan: Sometimes.

Mrs. L.: Good for you! See the letter *S* with the stars inside? That's a great hint about the first word of this rhyme, isn't it?

Class: *Star*!

Jack: *S-T-A-R*.

Mrs. L.: Do you see the word *star* anywhere else in the poem?

Ryan: I do. Right under the first *star*.

Mrs. L.: Great! Any guesses as to what *W-I-S-H* spells? Give the first sound, and think about what you do when you see the first star at night.

Brittany: Make a wish!

Mrs. L.: Wonderful! I wish you would read the rhyme with me now. *(We read the poem using the whisper-and-echo strategy. Then we reread the rhyme several times as I point to each word.)*

Jared: Can I come up and choose my favorite one? It's about nighttime, too. It's one of the last ones.

Mrs. L: Whisper the first line to me, and I'll find the rhyme in the index of first lines. Here it is. Let's show it to the class. What hints do you see?

Rachel: The first word starts with *W*.

Mrs. L.: Actually, the first three words start with *W*, and the words are this boy's name.

Blake: He's wearing his pajamas and holding a candle.

Megan: It's Wee Willie Winkle!

Mrs. L.: Close. He's Wee Willie Winkie. Let's whisper-and-echo this rhyme. *(We read the poem using the whisper-and-echo strategy.)* Great! Now, I'm going to divide you into four groups, and we'll read it like we're talking back and forth. *(I whisper the lines for each group to echo. Group 1: "Wee Willie Winkie runs through the town." Group 2: "Upstairs and downstairs in his night-gown." Group 3: "Rapping at the window, crying through the lock." Group 4: "Are the children all in bed, for now it's eight o'clock?")*

Jack: Can we do my favorite one now? It's "Hickory Dickory Dock."

Mrs. L.: That's always been one of my favorites, too. I have always said "Hickory, Dickory, Dock," too. But in this book it's "Dickory, Dickory, Dock." I think Mother Goose rhymes are sometimes different depending on who is retelling them. Let's read it together. *(We read the poem using the whisper-and-echo strategy.)* Good reading! I never knew there was a cat sleeping next to the clock. Did you?

Michael: The clock looks like a cat, too.

Mrs. L.:	I noticed that. I have an idea. Let's have this half of the class be clocks and say, "tick-tock, tick-tock, tick-tock" with a beat. It might help to sway to keep the beat. The rest of you say the rhyme with me. *(We repeat the rhyme, while half the class chants and sways to the beat.)*
Casey:	Let's do it again!
Mrs. L.:	Sure. Let's switch things around. Those who said the rhyme can be clocks this time. The clocks can say the rhyme. *(We repeat the rhyme, while the other half of the class sways to the beat.)* Nice job! I used to sing this when I was a child. In fact, many of Mother Goose's rhymes are songs.
Zachary:	I like "Baa, Baa, Black Sheep."
Mrs. L.:	Let's read it together. Please be my echo. *(We read the poem using the whisper-and-echo strategy.)*
Mrs. L.:	When Ryan and I read this together, we change the last line: "And one for the little boy who lives on—"
Ryan:	"Old Farm Lane."
Mrs. L.:	Old Farm Lane is the street we live on.
Rachel:	And Ryan is a little boy who lives on Old Farm Lane.
Mrs. L.:	Right. When Ryan's little sister came along, we had to change the words again. Now we say: "One for the little kids who live on Old Farm Lane." It's fun to change the words in a rhyme.
Zachary:	I like your poem.
Mrs. L.:	I think Mother Goose would, too. She'd be happy that we were playing with her words. Let's have a little more fun with Mother Goose.

5 More Great Mother Goose-Based Ideas

1. Make a letter and fill it with pictures beginning with the letter sound, for example, an *S* filled with stars as in "Star Light, Star Bright." (See the sample on page 23.)
2. Cut out goose shapes for children to record their favorite Mother Goose rhyme. Display as a graph of favorites or as a border for a bulletin board.
3. Set up a Play Dough center where students can make and bake food items to go with the many food-related poems.
4. Record rereadings by the class on audio- or videotape for a Mother Goose listening center.
5. Set up a rhyming word study center. Chart a few rhymes, and record rhyming word pairs on index cards. Let students match the words to the chart with Sticky-Tack.

More Must-Have Books of Read-Aloud Rhymes

Here Comes Mother Goose

edited by Iona Opie

Rhyming Words

For a double dose of Mother Goose rhymes interpreted by Iona Opie and Rosemary Wells, add *Here Comes Mother Goose* to your classroom bookshelf. The rhymes in this book are just right for paired readings. Chart this favorite.

Jelly on a plate,
Jelly on a plate,
Wibble, wobble, wibble, wobble,
Jelly on a plate.

Sausage in a pan,
Sausage in a pan.
Frizzle, frazzle, frizzle, frazzle,
Sausage in a pan.

After sharing the rhyme as it was written, copy the lines leaving blank spaces as shown below. Invite students to fill in the blanks to make a rhyme of their own. Reread their rhymes for more fluency practice.

________ *on a plate,*	*Pizza on a plate,*
________ *on a plate,*	*Pizza on a plate,*
________, ________,	*Pepperoni, pepperoni,*
________ *on a plate.*	*Pizza on a plate.*
________ *in a pan,*	*Bacon in a pan,*
________ *in a pan,*	*Bacon in a pan,*
________, ________, ________, ________,	*Sizzle, splatter, sizzle, splatter,*
________ *in a pan.*	*Bacon in a pan.*

Rich Vocabulary

fetch *v.* to bring

Mother Goose Read-Aloud Tips

- Read and reread the rhymes to become familiar with them.
- Choose a rhyme by opening the book to any page, or invite students to pick a favorite to read.

- As each new rhyme is chosen, have students gather hints from the illustrations to guess its title.
- Allow time for discussing the rhymes you share.
- Add rhythm instruments to get children involved in the rhythm of the language.

MEET THE ILLUSTRATOR: ROSEMARY WELLS

When discussing her illustrations for this book at a children's literature conference, Rosemary Wells explained that she intentionally added a little humor for the adults who would be sharing these classic rhymes with children. The cat with seven wives who rides to St. Ives looks amazingly similar to the one who loves Susannah best but also dances with the girl with the hole in her stocking. Is this fast-moving feline also Bonny Bobby Shaftoe who's gone to sea? Take a closer look and see for yourself!

MORE FUN WITH THE BOOK

Take a ride to St. Ives with the cat with seven wives, make some tarts with the queen of hearts, visit the cat with the measles, and ride a scooter to the fishmonger's with Old Mother Hubbard. Introduce your students to Dusty Bill from Vinegar Hill who never had a bath and never will. Copy these and other familiar rhymes onto chart paper, leaving spaces for students to fill in new words for sharing. With or without rhyming words, these silly rewrites will have preschoolers chanting the new twists on the classic rhymes in no time at all. Place a copy of *Here Comes Mother Goose* and the charted rhymes in a reading corner so children can reread the rhymes and look at the illustrations again and again.

Read-Aloud Rhymes for the Very Young

selected by Jack Prelutsky

Strengthening Oral Language

Before sharing the poems in this book with the children on your lap or in your classroom, read Jim Trelease's introduction for a reminder of why rhymes are so perfect for the great "listening machines" in your life.

> *Unlike the toys we buy our children, poems cannot break. Their flavor will last longer than a hundred boxes of candy. They come already assembled and need only one battery—a reader connected to one child. And that reader can start a glow that lasts a lifetime.*

Rich Vocabulary

sigh *v.* to make a sound that is soft like air

The 200 poems in this child-friendly collection were chosen exclusively for very young children who are wired with short attention spans. Who better to do the selecting than favorite children's poet Jack Prelutsky? Who better to illustrate the poems than Marc Brown? Who better to start a glow that lasts a lifetime than a preschool teacher, often a child's first role model for reading outside the home?

Keep *Read-Aloud Rhymes for the Very Young* close at hand for times when you have a few free minutes or you need a way to refocus students. Children will be relating to and talking about their own prior experiences and clamoring to try a few new ones. The discussions based on the kid-friendly poems in this collection are perfect for strengthening oral language development.

Use the index as your guide for introducing stimulating discussions of any number of learning themes such as the following

- Open a unit on insects by sharing poems like "Fuzzy Wuzzy, Creepy Crawly," "Ants," "Dragonfly," and "Grasshopper Green." Celebrate the first day of winter with "Dragon Smoke," and "The More It Snows."
- Extend the learning to a unit on seasons with "Happy Winter, Steamy Tub," "O Spring, O Spring," and "August Heat."
- Let "Ears Hear" and "Poor Shadow" kick off a discussion for a science unit on sound and light.

In addition, be ready to discuss squares on the kitchen floor, handle requests to blow bubbles and attempts to whistle, somersault, and to learn the naughty soap song. Simply put, this book lets kids be kids.

Wiggle Waggle Fun

by Margaret Mayo

Exploring the Beat of Poetry

In this collection of stories and rhymes for the very young, Margaret Mayo selected stories, poems, and rhymes for 24 talented artists to illustrate. The result is a favorite must-have book for every preschool classroom that is a feast for the eyes and ears.

Extend learning with rhyme-related movement exercises that let preschoolers explore the beat of rhyming texts. First, read a poem to your class, and then invite children to read along using the whisper-and-echo strategy (see page 9 of this book). Next, call on individuals to identify a form of movement for each poem. You can also link the following movements to poems:

- Form a line. Then make a train by placing hands on the hips of the person in front and move around the classroom to the beat of "Puff-puff, Choo-choo!"

Rich Vocabulary

pelting *v.* hitting against over and over

- Have children wiggle waggle their heads, shoulders, knees, and toes with "Wiggle Waggle and Crocodile Snap."
- March and stomp your feet to the beat of "Splishy-Sploshy Wet Day."
- Break out the rhythm instruments for "Boom! Boom! Oomm-pah-pah!"

Every page of this great book invites involvement as children wiggle-waggle, listen-discuss, splash-splosh, boom-boom, and toot-toot their way through the read-it-again stories, poems, and rhymes.

Tomie dePaola's Mother Goose

by Tomie dePaola

LEARNING ABOUT **How Print Is Organized**

> **Rich Vocabulary**
>
> **speckled** *adj.* covered with spots

When sharing this collection of Mother Goose rhymes with preschoolers, take time to compare Tomie dePaola's drawings for "Humpty Dumpty," "Old King Cole," and "Bobby Shaftoe" with Rosemary Wells' illustrations of these same characters. A few sharp listeners will be quick to point out word variations in DePaola's and Opie's rhymes such as "Hickory Dickory Dock," "Three Men in a Tub," and "1, 2, Buckle My Shoe."

Set up a Mother Goose center of activities based on this book. Provide a reading area where students can take a closer look at Mother Goose books shared for read-aloud. (Look for the board book of *Tomie dePaola's Mother Goose.*) Invite children to bring Mother Goose books from home.

For extra fun, include activities for individual rhymes such as those listed below. Chart each rhyme to display at the center, and then provide individual baskets of materials for each poem.

"1, 2, Buckle My Shoe"

Collect objects for children to use as props to retell the rhyme: a shoe that buckles, a few small twigs, a toy or paper door, and a toy hen. As students reread the rhyme, encourage them to point to each word to reinforce the left-to-right flow of words.

Make a copy of the rhyme on page 22 for each student. Cut each rhyme into strips, and scramble them. Ask students to place strips in order from 1 to 10 and then glue them onto construction paper.

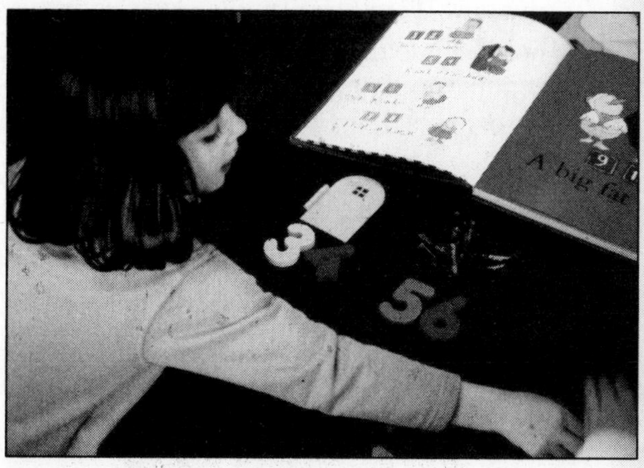

Playing at the Mother Goose center

"Star Light, Star Bright"
Distribute copies of the reproducible on page 23 to students. Challenge children to find all the *S*'s in the rhyme. Then have them cover the *S* at the bottom of the page with small foil star stickers. As children read the poem, ask them to hold up their *S* each time they see the letter.

"Humpty Dumpty"
For an egg-stra special word study, use plastic eggs filled with words and letters for students to explore. Fill each of four eggs with one line of the poem for them to place in order. You can also fill each of 12 eggs with a magnetic letter to spell so they can spell *H-U-M-P-T-Y D-U-M-P-T-Y.*

"Good Morning Mrs. Hen"
Provide crayons or markers and copies of the reproducible on page 24 so students can color the hens as described in the rhyme: four yellow, four brown, two speckled red.

Sheep in a Jeep
by Nancy Shaw

LEARNING ABOUT Rhyming Words

Poor sheep. First their jeep gets stuck on a hill that's steep. When they push the jeep off the hill, it gets stuck in the mud at the bottom. They enlist the help of two tough, tattooed pigs who help them tug the jeep out of the mud—only to crash it into a tree. To make a short story shorter: Jeep in a heap. Sheep weep. Jeep for sale—cheap.

Get extra mileage out of this book about sheep and their jeep with an introduction to rhyming words. Display the cover with the sheep in a jeep, and write the word *sheep* on the board. Erase the *sh*, and add a *j* for *jeep*. Then erase the *j* and add a *b* for *beep*. Reread the story, pointing out how the illustrations follow the text with words that "sound the same" on each page.

To simplify this introductory illustration of rhyming words, you may wish to use sound-spelling so all the words look alike as I did. Write each word, and then erase the beginning to show how the rhyming words sound and look alike (the crossed-out letters in the sample on the next page represent erased letters). Continue with other rhyming words in the book.

Rich Vocabulary

steep *adj*. tall to climb (like a hill)

heap *n*. a pile

~~sh~~eep	*~~gr~~unt*	*~~th~~ud*	*~~t~~ug*	*~~y~~elp*	*out*	*~~ch~~eer*
~~j~~eep	*~~fr~~unt*	*~~m~~ud*	*~~sh~~rug*	*~~h~~elp*	*~~sh~~out*	*~~d~~eer*
~~b~~eep						*~~st~~eer*
~~st~~eep						
~~l~~eep						
~~h~~eep						
~~w~~eep						
~~ch~~eep						

Next, take a word such as *tug*, and make a list of your own rhyming words. This time, write the part that is the same on the board, and ask students to add a beginning letter to make new words—both nonsense and real words. You may wish to start at *A* and work your way through to *Z*—from *bug* to *zug*!

Tumble Bumble

by Felicia Bond

Combining Words and Movement

A tiny bug went for a walk.
He met a cat and stopped to talk.
They fell in step and strolled a while,
and bumped into a crocodile.
— From *Tumble Bumble*, pages 3–4

Grab *Tumble Bumble*, and let your students take "a walk on the wild side." The charming illustrations and catchy rhyming text make this a great book to read again and again with preschoolers. Felicia Bond's mouse from *If You Give a Mouse a Cookie* (Laura Numeroff, 1985) and pig from *If You Give a Pig a Pancake* (Laura Numeroff, 1998) make an encore appearance with a host of new friends as they tumble bumble their way to exhaustion and into a little boy's bed for a short rest before tumble bumbling again.

Allow your active preschoolers to put their extra energy to good use with this book-based movement activity. Have them make a circle around you. As you reread *Tumble Bumble*, children can do the Tumble Bumble with a few easy dance steps that follow the rollicking text.

Rich Vocabulary

introduced *v.* met someone new

Do the Tumble Bumble

- fall in step (left, right, left, right)
- stroll awhile (slide your feet)
- dance a jig (dance in place)
- bounce along (hop, hop)
- zigzag down the road (twist, step, twist, step)
- tippy-toe (tip-toe, tip-toe with finger to lips—sshhh)

For added fun, tell students to stop each time an animal bumps into a new friend. They can grin wide with glee, introduce a bee, apologize to a pig, sing a song, blow a kiss, ring the doorbell, look for something good to eat, tumble bumble up the stairs, and open doors to check for bears while moving around the room.

Mr. Brown Can Moo! Can You?

by Dr. Seuss

LEARNING ABOUT Exploring Sounds

Oh the wonderful things
Mr. Brown can do!
MOO MOO
BUZZ BUZZ
POP POP POP
EEK EEK
HOO HOO
KLOPP KLOPP KLOPP. . .

— From *Mr. Brown Can Moo! Can You?*, page 28

Rich Vocabulary

slurp *v.* to make noise while drinking

This book invites a chorus of responses from preschoolers who are naturally impressed by Mr. Brown's ability to imitate every kind of sound imaginable. From the "dibble dibble dopp" of the rain and the "grum grum grum" of a hippopotamus chewing gum to the "pip" of a goldfish kiss, your children will love making these and other new sounds of their own.

Read this great book to children, and talk about how the words used are extra special because Dr. Seuss had to invent them. Invite students to make each sound with you as you read, discuss favorite sounds, and then provide a little book-based science exploration.

Chart the wonderful noisy words from the story next to a box filled with noisemakers and other items to create a sound center where students can explore these noises and other sounds that Mr. Brown made.

Sound-Making Items for Mr. Brown's Sound Center

- blocks of wood for knocking
- sandpaper for sizzling
- bells for ringing
- noisemakers for all kinds of sounds
- rhythm sticks for klopping
- whistles for blowing
- winding clocks for a tick-tock sound
- musical instruments (toy trumpet, harmonica, xylophone, drum, maracas, tambourine)
- animal "sound" shakers (small tins that students shake to make animal noises)
- straws and cups of water for bubbling, gurgling noises (Remind students to dispose of straws after placing them in their mouths.)
- paper cups connected with strings for whisper exploration
- OPTIONAL: earplugs for teacher!

Is Your Mama a Llama?

by Deborah Guarino

Listening Skills

"Is your mama a llama?" I asked my friend Dave.
"No, she is not," is the answer Dave gave.
"She hangs by her feet, and she lives in a cave.
I do not believe that's how llamas behave."
"Oh," I said. "You are right about that.
I think that your mama sounds more like a . . . Bat!"

— From *Is Your Mama a Llama?*, pages 6–10

> **Rich Vocabulary**
>
> **politely** *adv.* nicely; with good manners

This must-have book was inspired by Deborah Guarino's introduction to a real mama llama at the zoo. In this rhyming riddle story, Lloyd the llama meets many other animals who characterize their mamas with distinct details: One mama grazes on grass and likes to say "moo"; another has whiskers and flippers; another has a long neck, white feathers and wings—can you guess who is who?

For a lesson that sharpens listening skills, read the story without showing the pictures to students. Have them listen carefully to the story clues in order to chime in with the correct mama animal's name. Read the story again, this time revealing the pictures for all to see.

Following the read-aloud, allow time for each student to draw a picture of his or her mama, other caregiver, or mama animal from the story and dictate a sentence. As an alternate activity, provide nature magazines so students can cut out pictures of mama and baby animals for a collage.

"My Mama smiles at me."

Maddie, age 4

"Mommy and me are holding hands."

Ryan, age 6

Jamberry
by Bruce Degan

Letter Sounds

One berry
Two berry
Pick me a blueberry
Hatberry
Shoeberry
In my canoeberry
— From *Jamberry*, pages 2–4

When a boy meets a friendly bear who offers him a ride in a canoe and a hat full of blueberries, there's no telling what will hap-

Rich Vocabulary

meadows *n.* fields of grass

pen next! Together the bear and the boy enter a berry-filled world where the flowers are made of cookies, trees have sliced bread leaves, and marshmallow-tipped bushes are ready to be picked. Preschoolers' imaginations go wild as the canoe tumbles over a waterfall of blueberries.

This delightful, romping, read-aloud rhyme is sure to have students chanting along! Use the great *Jamberry* words for a lesson on beginning, middle and ending letter clues. On index cards, copy the words from the book with *b-e-r-r-y* in them. Display the words in scrambled order in your gathering space.

jamberry	*pawberry*	*razzamatazzberry*
berry	*quickberry*	*berryband*
blueberry	*quackberry*	*Berryland*
hatberry	*blackberry*	*brassberry*
shoeberry	*trainberry*	*moonberry*
canoeberry	*trackberry*	*starberry*
berries	*clickety-clackberry*	*cloudberry*
hayberry	*raspberry*	*boomberry*
strawberry	*jazzberry*	*zoomberry*

Using the title as an example, say, "J-j-j-jamberry." Ask students to identify the word *jamberry* by choosing the only word card that begins with *j* and has an *m* in the middle.

Read the story again, leaving out the berry words for students to fill in orally. Invite individual students to identify the correct berry word from the index cards, highlight the berry part, and place the cards in a bucket. When all the words have been identified, add the *Jamberry* book to the bucket, and you have a berry word picking center that is easily transported around the room for independent reading and word identification practice.

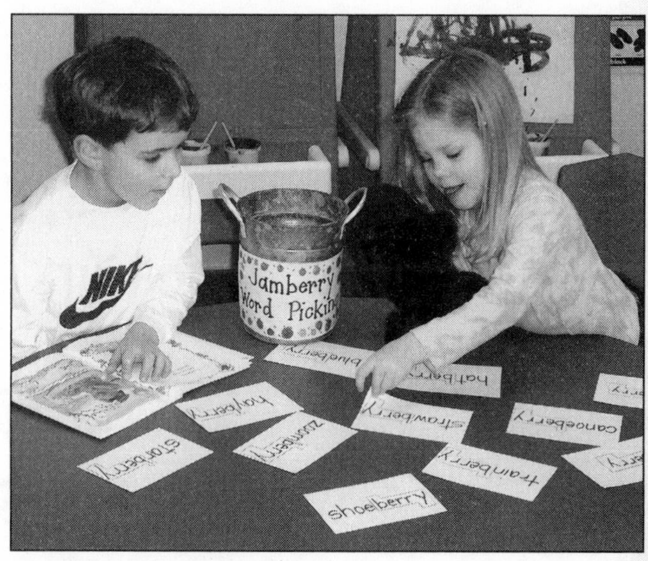

Our *Jamberry* word picking center

Even More Must-Have Books of Read-Aloud Rhymes

Hey Diddle Diddle and Other Mother Goose Rhymes by Tomie dePaola

Mother Goose: A Collection of Classic Nursery Rhymes selected and illustrated by Michael Hague

Kittycat Lullaby Rhymes by Eileen Spinelli

Sheep in a Shop by Nancy Shaw

Polar Bear, Polar Bear, What Do You Hear? by Bill Martin Jr. and John Archambault

Here Are My Hands by Bill Martin Jr.

Go Dog, Go! by P.D. Eastman

Babushka's Mother Goose by Patricia Polacco

Animal Crackers Nursery Rhymes by Jane Dyer

1, 2, Buckle My Shoe

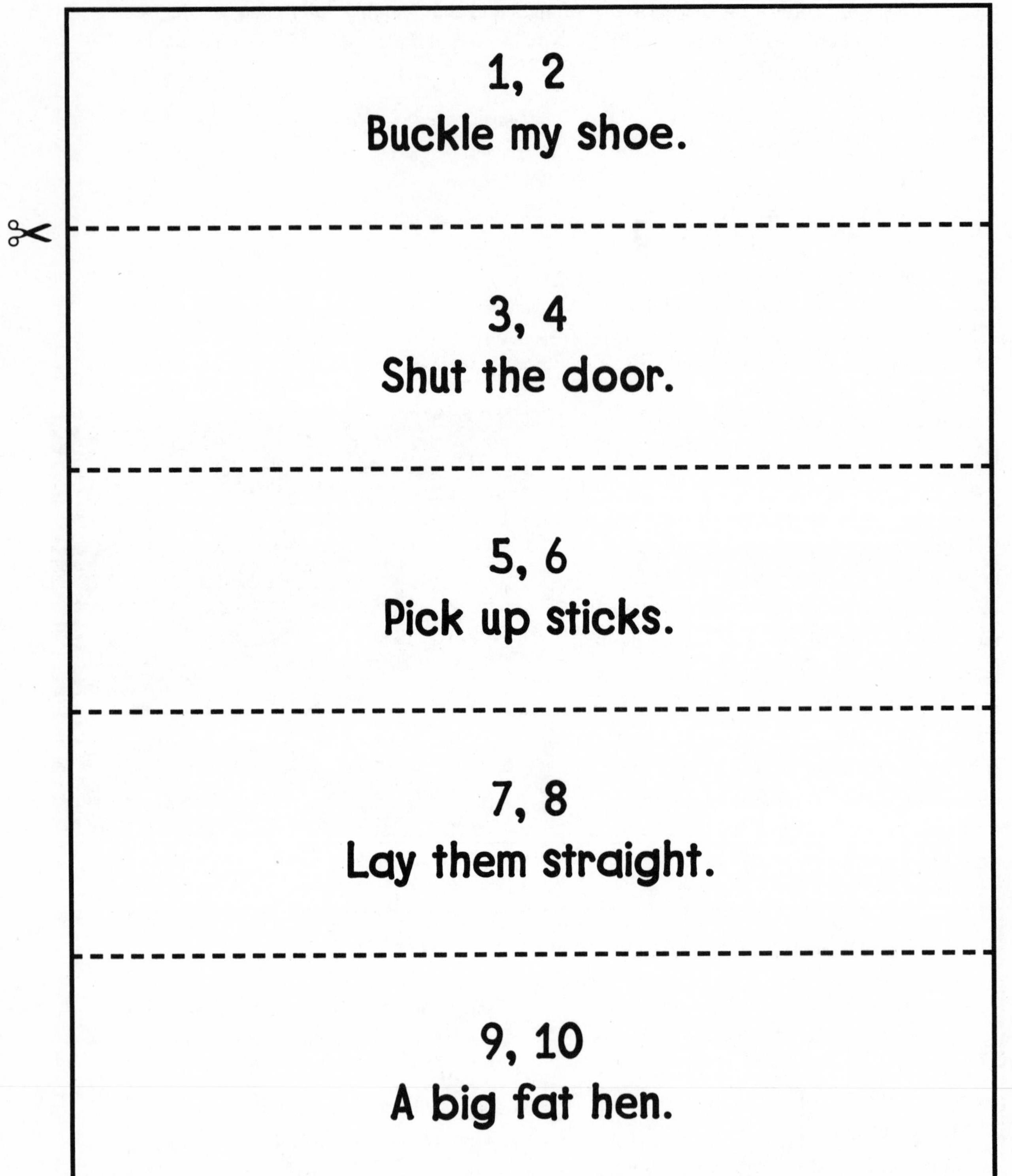

1, 2
Buckle my shoe.

3, 4
Shut the door.

5, 6
Pick up sticks.

7, 8
Lay them straight.

9, 10
A big fat hen.

Use with *Tomie dePaola's Mother Goose.*

Name ______________________________ Date ____________________

Star Light, Star Bright

Circle each S.

Star light, star bright
First star I see tonight,
I wish I may, I wish I might,
Have the wish I wish tonight.

Cover the S with stars.

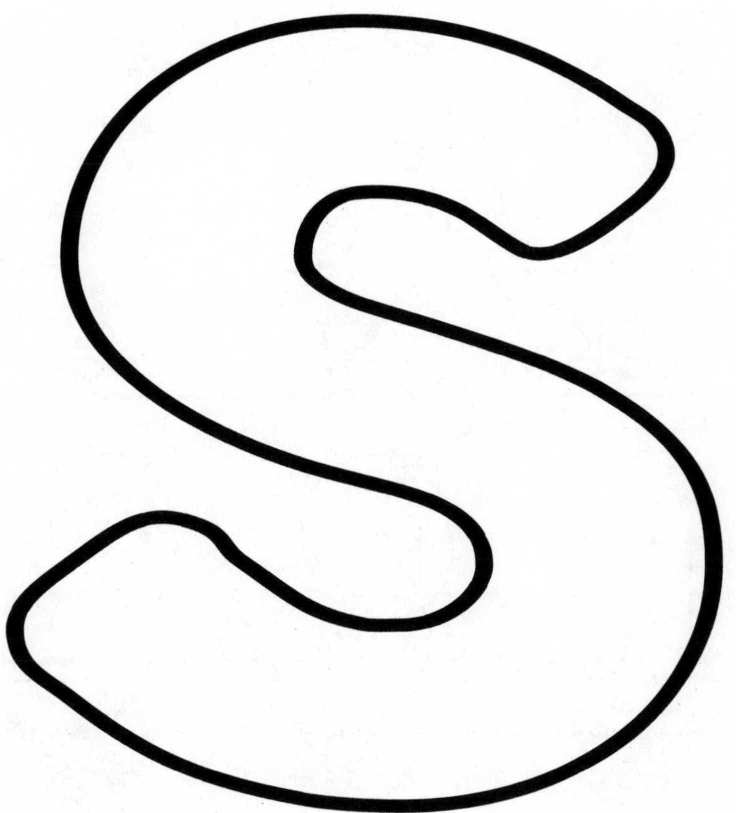

Use with *Tomie dePaola's Mother Goose.*

Name ______________________________ Date ____________________

Good Morning, Mrs. Hen

Listen to the rhyme.
Color the chicks to match the words.

Chook, chook, chook, chook, chook,
Good morning, Mrs. Hen.
How many chickens have you got?
Madam, I've got ten.
Four of them are yellow,
And four of them are brown.
And two of them are speckled red,
The nicest in the town.

Use with *Tomie dePaola's Mother Goose.*

Chapter 2: A Book for Any Kind of Day

10 Must-Have Books About Feelings and Events In Our Everyday Lives

Chapter Learning Goals:

- identifying feelings and positive ways to express them
- relating to the feelings of others through books
- strengthening oral language
- building listening skills
- writing about feelings

A book is a wonderful way for parents to reconnect with children after a long day of work and school. Teachers and students often need to reconnect, too. Books can bring your class back together with a focus after a special event or recess. The must-have books in this chapter are perfect for helping students understand feelings and observing and discussing them through the actions of book characters. These books are also perfect for stimulating discussions about feelings and exploring the range of emotions in preschoolers.

Help children learn to handle anger with *When Sophie Gets Angry—Really, Really Angry*.... Be a "moodsketeer" with *Today I Feel Silly and Other Moods That Make My Day*. When it's one of those time-out, wear-you-out kind of days, students will relate to talking things over with *Olivia*. Talk about things we all worry about after reading *Wemberly Worried*. Use *Morris's Disappearing Bag* to talk about those days when we'd like to disappear. Let *The Everything Book* lead to the expression of different emotions through pictures and words. Encourage everyone to feel gray, yellow, red, and blue with Dr. Seuss's *My Many Colored Days*. No matter the weather, reading *The Snowy Day* will unfreeze children's snowy-day imaginations. Students will respond to the loving relationships in *Oh My Baby, Little One*. And when boredom strikes your classroom, read *Pete's a Pizza*.

10 Must-Have Books for Any Kind of Day

When Sophie Gets Angry—Really, Really Angry . . . by Molly Bang

Today I Feel Silly and Other Moods That Make My Day by Jamie Lee Curtis

Olivia by Ian Falconer

Wemberly Worried by Kevin Henkes

Morris's Disappearing Bag by Rosemary Wells

The Everything Book by Denise Fleming

My Many Colored Days by Dr. Seuss

The Snowy Day by Ezra Jack Keats

Oh My Baby, Little One by Kathi Appelt

Pete's a Pizza by William Steig

A a B b C c B b A a C c

MINI-LESSON IN ACTION

When Sophie Gets Angry—Really, Really Angry . . .

by Molly Bang

LEARNING ABOUT Handling Anger

She kicks. She screams. She wants to smash the world to smithereens. She roars a red, red roar. Sophie is a volcano, ready to explode.

— From *When Sophie Gets Angry—Really, Really Angry . . .*, pages 9–12

The result *is* often similar to a volcano when anger and a preschooler meet. As Sophie's sister grabs Gorilla, Sophie sees red. Like many preschoolers, her temper tantrum involves kicking, roaring, and screaming. Then Sophie deals with her anger in a unique way: "She runs and runs and runs until she can't run anymore." Sophie cries for a little while before climbing her favorite tree where "the wide world comforts her."

Let Sophie's experiences set the stage for a discussion that proves everyone gets angry, that people handle anger in different ways, and most important, that there are appropriate ways to handle "red hot anger." Sophie's story will get students talking about the following:

- times they've been so mad they wanted to smash the world to smithereens
- what comforts them when they're ready to explode
- what can be done to get "everything back together again" for a happy ending like Sophie's

Our classroom discussion of what happens when we get really, really angry goes something like this.

Rich Vocabulary

snatched *v.* took quickly without asking

Mrs. L.: We all get really, really angry sometimes. What did Sophie do when her sister grabbed Gorilla from her?

Rachel: Tried to grab it back.

Blake: That's when she fell over the truck.

Megan: That's what made Sophie really, really angry.

Mrs. L.: Let me show you the picture of Sophie when she's really, really angry.

Ryan: It looks just like the cover of the book.

Mrs. L.: You're right. Show me your really, really angry face. Wow—what angry kids! Tell me what Sophie did when she got mad.

Ben: She roared like a dragon.

Mrs. L.: Yes, the book says, "she roared a red, red roar." What else?

Brittany: She kicked her feet.

Ryan: She wanted to smash up the world!

Jared: Right—to smash the world to smithereens!

Mrs. L: Then what did Sophie do?

Casey: Ran and ran and ran and ran.

Rebecca: She cried, too.

Michael: She got to her favorite tree and climbed it, and then she looked around.

Mrs. L.: Let me read the words on the next few pages: "She feels the breeze blow her hair. She watches the water and the waves. The wide world comforts her."

Victoria: She felt better then.

Michael: She went back home and everything was happy again.

Mrs. L.: Let's look back at the page where Sophie's mad. How does this page make you feel?

Rachel: Mad with Sophie.

Mrs. L.: Now look at this page where she says, "I'm home . . . "

Casey: That page makes me smile.

Brittany: Everyone's happy again—even the cat.

Tommy: Look at the cat on the angry page.

Blake: He looks scared.

Mrs. L.: I agree. The words on the page when Sophie arrives home again are "the house is warm and smells good. Everyone is glad she's home."

Megan: That makes me feel happy for Sophie.

Mrs. L.: I love the last two pages where "everything's back together again."

Ryan: Just like the puzzle.

Mrs. L.: Exactly!

Ben: And Sophie paints a picture with smiles on the faces.

Jack: And the tree she climbs with the world around her.

Mrs. L.: What a happy ending. The next time you're angry, think of Sophie and remember that eventually, the angry feeling will go away. What we do to make the anger go away is important. Sophie didn't hit her sister or push her.

Ryan: I bet she wanted to.

Mrs. L.: Maybe, but she made a decision to handle her anger in her own way.

Megan: By running and running and running.

Mrs. L.: Yes. Pretend you're playing with your favorite toy. Your brother or sister or a friend grabs it from you. What would you do?

Zachary: I'd chase her and grab it back.

Mrs. L.: What if your mom said, "Zach, it's her turn now"—like Sophie's mom said to her?

Zachary: Then I'd tell her it's my favorite toy, and I don't want to share it.

Jack: Or you could both play with it.

Mrs. L.: That's a nice idea.

Michael: My mom tells me I'm not allowed to take something from my little brother unless I have something to give him to play with.

Mrs. L.: Sophie probably would have felt better if her sister had traded something with her instead of just grabbing Gorilla.

Ryan: My mom always tells me to use my words.

Mrs. L.: What words would you use?

Ryan: I was playing with that first. I'll let you use it in one minute or two.

Mrs. L.: Those would be kind words to use. But when you're in the middle of feeling really, really, angry . . .

Ryan: I'd say, "Hey! GIVE THAT BACK!"

Casey: I pushed my sister, Jordan, one time when she grabbed a book from me.

Michael: I hit my brother for taking my truck.

Mrs. L.: Did those actions make the person want to give the toy back?

Michael: No, it made my brother mad, too.

Ryan: If I say nicely, "Maddie, please give that back," she sometimes does.

Mrs. L.: But it is hard to find nice words when you're really, really angry. What you need is called self-control. It's reaching deep inside yourself for kind words and actions. We all get angry and say and do things we don't mean. Part of growing up is using self-control.

Blake: My mom tells me to count to ten when I get really angry before I do anything. She says that might make me feel better. Sometimes it does.

Mrs. L.: Counting to ten is a great way to gather up your self-control. Sophie could have counted to ten. But she found that running to her favorite tree and letting the wide world comfort her is her way of getting control. What other things do you do when you're angry? What might you do to get control the next time you're really, really angry? I'll write your ideas down on a chart.

When We Get Angry—Really, Really Angry . . .
Brittany lies on her bed and hugs her bear.
Ryan punches his pillow or talks to his dog.
Blake counts to ten and then uses nice words.
Victoria stomps her feet.
Jared growls like a bear and then uses his words kindly.
Michael hides until the anger is gone.
Rebecca cries and cries and cries. Then her mom gets her giggling again.
Ben shakes his fists and makes a mean face.
Jack screams really loud—inside his head.
Rachel used to throw things. Now she runs to her room.
Tommy runs to his mom for a hug.
Megan likes to scribble on paper.
Casey used to bite when he was little. Now he uses his words.
Zachary used to chase the person he was mad at. Now he uses his words, too.

ON ANOTHER DAY

We practice using anger appropriately by role-playing anger-inducing situations.

Role-Playing Scenarios

- You're playing with your favorite toy. Your sister grabs it from you.
- Your friend asks to take a turn on your brand new bike. You say, "Sure." When the turn is over, he refuses to give the bike back and keeps on riding.
- You're playing ball. Your friend pushes you out of the way to catch it.
- You're playing at a friend's house. He says that since it's his house, he gets to decide what to play.
- There's one cookie left in the cookie jar for you and a friend to share. Your friend says she is hungrier than you and eats the whole cookie in one bite.
- You want everything to be "back together again." Use your words so everyone feels better: "I'm sorry," "I accept your apology," "Let's hug."

Role-playing with Sophie

MORE FUN WITH THE BOOK

- Place a copy of *When Sophie Gets Angry—Really, Really Angry . . .* in a basket next to the time-out area. Let Sophie's red hot anger serve as a reminder that everyone gets angry.
- Rehearse the role-playing scenarios, and then record them on videotape. Provide props so students can reenact the scenes with different solutions. They can watch their performances during free time.

More Must-Have Books for Any Kind of Day

Today I Feel Silly and Other Moods That Make My Day

by Jamie Lee Curtis

From silly to grumpy, angry to joyful, and confused to lonely and frustrated, Jamie Lee Curtis knows all about the range of emotions that typify the preschool years. Each page of this book allows students and teachers to explore a different emotion with rhyming text and humorous, detailed illustrations.

On the "Today I am sad" page, the young narrator admits that she and her best friend had a really big fight. "She said that I tattled and I know that she's right." The accompanying illustration is a photo album open to a page showing a photo of the two friends. An uncapped black marker lying nearby explains the black mustache and *x*'s covering the narrator's best friend.

And preschoolers unanimously agree with the ending rhyme.

> *I'd rather feel silly, excited or glad,*
> *than cranky or grumpy, discouraged or sad.*
> *But moods are just something that happen each day.*
> *Whatever I'm feeling inside is okay!* (page 27)

But the best feature of this book is yet to come. After this final rhyme, the last page boasts two wheels that spin to change the facial expressions of the little girl from silly to happy, excited, cranky, sad, or angry. Children turn the word wheel to answer the question, "How do YOU feel today?"

After discussing the many moods that make up our day, allow students to gauge their varying emotions by making individual Feelings Wheels using copies of pages 39 and 40. After they add details such as eye color and hair to page 40 with crayons, assist them in cutting out the mouth and making a slit on the dotted lines. Then have them color and cut out the wheel on page 39, and help them secure it under the face with a paper fastener.

As you reread the story, ask students to adjust their wheels to

Rich Vocabulary

frustrated *v.* not being able to finish or do something

match the feelings being described. Place a Feelings Wheel as well as a copy of *Today I Feel Silly and Other Moods That Make My Day* at the time-out corner for use as needed.

Today I feel . . . angry.

Olivia

by Ian Falconer

Listening and Speaking Skills

As her mother puts Olivia to bed after another long day, she gives her daughter a kiss and says, "You know, you really wear me out. But I love you anyway." And Olivia gives her mother a kiss back and says, "I love you anyway too."

Olivia, with her strong-willed tendencies and dreams of performing on the stage, has a large preschool following. Whether it's the debate over how many books to read at bedtime, painting a mural on the wall after a trip to the art museum, or having to be firm with a younger sibling, every preschooler will identify in some way with Olivia.

This Caldecott Honor book makes a perfect read-aloud for rainy days, sunny days, time-out days, or any day. And, given how much your children will have in common with Olivia, this book will provide opportunities for them to hone their speaking and listening skills as they participate in a literary discussion of the book.

A Book Talk with *Olivia*

- Olivia lives with her mother, father, little brother, dog and cat. Tell about your family.
- Every morning, Olivia brushes her teeth, combs her ears, and moves the cat. What do you do every morning?
- Olivia likes to go to the museum on rainy days. What do you like to do on rainy days?
- Olivia has a time-out for painting on the wall. Tell about a time-out you remember.

Rich Vocabulary

prepared *v.* being ready

- Olivia gets very good at building sand castles. What is your favorite thing to do at the beach?
- When it's time for her "you-know-what," Olivia is not sleepy. How do you feel about naps?
- Olivia dreams of singing and dancing on stage. What do you dream of doing someday?
- Olivia wants to read five books at bedtime. Mother says one. They settle on three. How many books do you usually read at bedtime?

Wemberly Worried

by Kevin Henkes

LEARNING ABOUT Relating to a Character's Feelings

What if no one else wears stripes?
What if no one else brings a doll?
What if the teacher is mean?
What if they make fun of my name?
What if I can't find the bathroom?
What if the room smells bad?
What if I hate the snack?
What if I have to cry?

— From *Wemberly Worried*, pages 20–22

Many preschoolers, like Wemberly, are predisposed to excessive worrying. Blessed with blossoming imaginations, the possible "what-ifs" of new situations can be overwhelming and cause great concern. Fortunately, Wemberly meets Jewel. Wearing stripes and holding their dolls, Jewel and Wemberly worry through the first day of school together.

This book by favorite author Kevin Henkes is perfect for the beginning of a new school year when uncertainties about school routines and making friends abound. On a worrying kind of day, preschool children can take comfort in how quickly and successfully Wemberly adapted to school.

After you read aloud the story, have children talk about Wemberly's worries and a few of their own to illustrate the fact that we all worry. Share some concerns of your own. Discuss ways to work together to ease each other's concerns and how to be sensitive to other people's feelings. Assure students that, like Wemberly, they will be smiling and "taking things as they come" in no time at all.

End the read-aloud and discussion time by showing the book cover, which depicts a very worried Wemberly clutching her doll, Petal. Invite

Rich Vocabulary

worried *v.* not feeling comfortable about something

students to bring in a favorite "comfort" item from home to share. Take photos of individuals holding a bear, doll, blanket or even a picture of Mom or Dad. Display the snapshots on a bulletin board for those times when a little extra comfort is needed.

Morris's Disappearing Bag

by Rosemary Wells

Strengthening Oral Language

When Morris finds one last present under the tree on Christmas Day, he opens it and disappears—inside his new disappearing bag. Now Morris has something his brothers and sisters want to play with, too. This must-have book is terrific for discussing feelings of jealousy and anger and sharing with others. Preschool audiences will want to hear this book over and over again as Rosemary Wells portrays the sentiments of many preschool students in the guise of an irresistible rabbit named Morris whose eyes and ears reveal his feelings without words.

Share this book, and then pretend to distribute "invisible bags" to each of your students. Have them close their eyes, disappear inside their bags, and pretend to be invisible. After everyone "reappears," talk about the times they would find this gift most useful.

If I had an invisible bag I would . . .

- use it for playing hide and seek. —Ryan
- go inside it during nap time. —Casey
- find my disappearing bag when we have broccoli for dinner. —Zach
- put my baby brother in it whenever he was taking my favorite toys. —Megan

One child's idea will lead to another as students think of endless reasons to put invisible bags on their wish lists. Don't forget to save a bag for yourself—when your preschoolers start to lose control, crawl inside with a warning that you'll come back out as soon as things are "calm" again or for Christmas—whichever comes first!

Rich Vocabulary

invented *v.* made something that was your own idea

The Everything Book

by Denise Fleming

LEARNING ABOUT **Depicting Emotions**

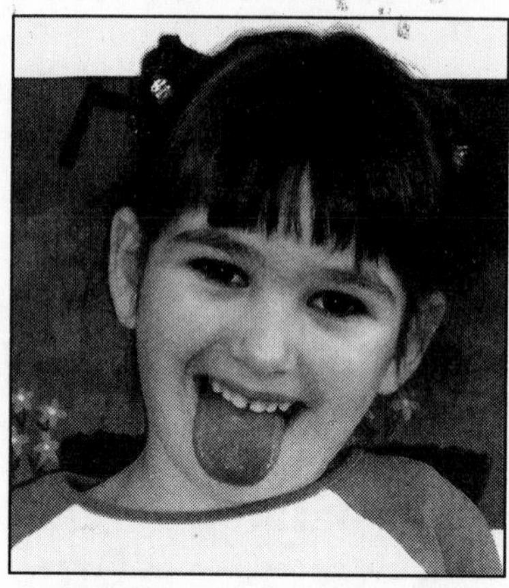

Yuck! Eew!

The Everything Book lives up to its title. A wonderful picture book resource for every preschool classroom, it has something for everyone. Denise Fleming created the illustrations for her books by "pouring colored cotton pulp through hand-cut stencils. The result—images set in handmade paper." And a book filled with vivid pages of motivating pictures that students pore over again and again.

We use the book to explore emotions and corresponding facial expressions by constructing a bulletin board of faces. Review "Faces" on pages 50 and 51 of *The Everything Book*, and then provide small mirrors for students to explore expressions such as "Yuck!," "Eew!," "Oh, no!," "Humph!," "Ha! ha!," and "Huh?" Use a Polaroid or digital camera to capture a few of these expressions. Ask students to decorate a piece of background paper for the photo with illustrations and a dictated or sound-spelled word that describes their emotional portrait. Display the portraits on the bulletin board for all to enjoy.

Oh no!

MORE FUN WITH THE BOOK

Naming Body Parts (pages 44–45)

Challenge students to identify body parts from head to toe on these pages. Introduce the song "Head, Shoulders, Knees and Toes," and then make an audio recording for students to listen to and sing along with at a listening center. For added head-to-toe practice, include a reading of Bill Martin Jr. and John Archambault's *Here Are My Hands* on the tape. End the tape by directing students to find their eyebrows, knees, thumbs, wrists, elbows, ankles, chests, and other "tricky" body parts.

Rich Vocabulary

confused *v.* not understanding something

Favorite Things Page (pages 52–55)

Using copies of the reproducible on page 41, interview students regarding their favorite things. After recording individual responses, have them illustrate one or more of their favorite things. (See page 53 for alphabet and counting activities for this book.)

My Many Colored Days

by Dr. Seuss

LEARNING ABOUT Expressing Feelings

Dr. Seuss (whose real name was Theodore Geisel) wrote this book in 1973, but it wasn't published until after his death when his wife, Audrey Geisel, brought the text to the attention of her late husband's editor. On the jacket she writes:

> *Ted had a panoramic view of ocean and land from his study, and he found the constantly changing patterns of light and color fascinating. He liked to compare the "mood," or color, of the day to his own emotional barometer setting. Though his inspiration for this book was personal, he felt that someone else should bring his or her own vision to it. He wanted the illustrations to be very different from his.*

The illustrators, Steve Johnson and Lou Fancher, have created a playful and bright complement to Dr. Seuss's words as well as a means of helping preschool children find words and images to describe the feelings of their many colored days.

When my son, Ryan, handed me the brightly painted shape shown at the left after preschool one day, I knew exactly what book his teacher, Miss Christy, had read that day. The colors red and yellow represented his mood that day and the words were added with markers.

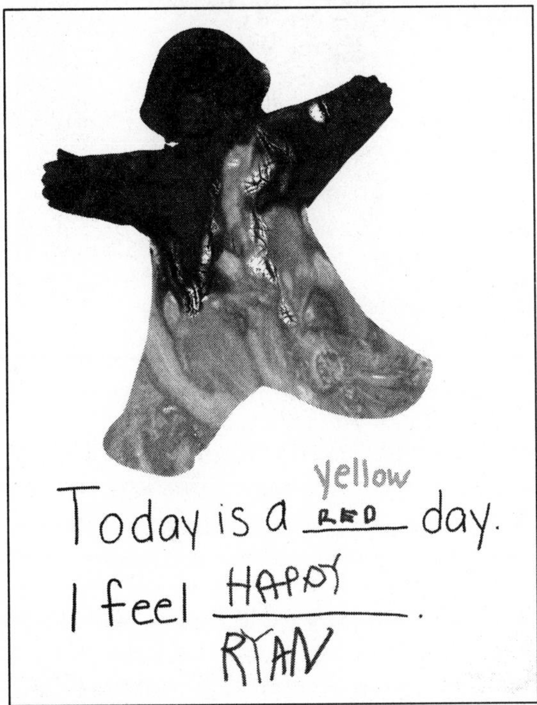

Ryan's yellow red day

Rich Vocabulary

groan *v.* to complain in a low, growly voice

Thinking of moods in relation to colors is a great way to get preschoolers to express their feelings in words. Although red was a day to feel good and "to be a horse and kick my heels" to Ryan and Dr. Seuss, students Megan and Casey, felt angry on bright red days. However we describe our feelings, the impact of this book is in its ability to help children step back, take a look at their moods, and adjust their actions accordingly. Black days when we're "mad and loud" require more self control, for example, than bright blue days when "I flap my wings."

After reading aloud *My Many Colored Days*, provide body-shaped outlines for students to paint to match their mood. Help them find the words to express their mood of the day, and write the words under the colored body shapes. Share your many colored days as a class.

The Snowy Day

by Ezra Jack Keats

LEARNING ABOUT Experiencing a Snowy Day

When Peter wakes up to discover that snow has fallen during the night and covered everything as far as he can see, he eats breakfast, puts on his snowsuit, and runs outside. This classic book is a favorite of preschool children who are eager for a day to play in the snow like Peter. And, if snowy days aren't an option in your area, this book provides children with an opportunity to join Peter as he investigates one particularly snowy day.

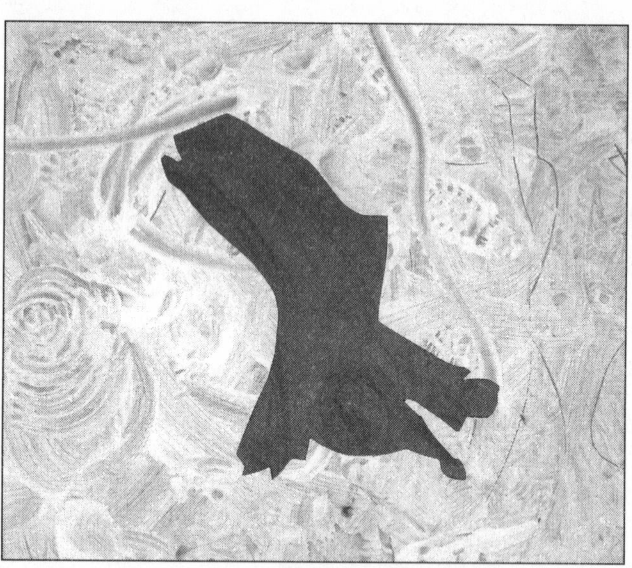

On snowy days I like to ______.

After reading aloud *The Snowy Day*, I introduce a snowy day center with a 3-Step Snowy Day art project. First, students paint a blue piece of paper with a white snowy hill as shown on the title page. I provide toothpicks and small doll shoes for making drag marks and footprints as Peter walks with his toes pointing in and out, drags his feet s-l-o-w-l-y to make tracks, and uses a stick to make a new track.

Next, students add a cutout of Peter (made prior to lesson by parent volunteers) and use a rubberstamp, Q-Tip, or fingertip to make snowflakes falling from the blue construction paper sky. Have them dictate or sound-spell a sentence describing their favorite ways to spend a snowy day.

> **Rich Vocabulary**
>
> **adventures** *n.* exciting events or activities

ON ANOTHER DAY

• For a book-based science lesson, place paper cups filled with ice cubes in various places around the classroom (in a closet, near a sunny windowsill, in an insulated lunch bag, or in a pocket like Peter did), and take estimates on rates of melting.

- Display a basket of more great books by Ezra Jack Keats such as those listed at the right for students to independently peruse during free time.

Other Great Books by Ezra Jack Keats

Pet Show
Hi, Cat!
A Letter to Amy
Whistle for Willie
Peter's Chair
Goggles!
Louie
The Trip
Apt. 3
Regards to the Man in the Moon
Dreams

Oh My Baby, Little One

by Kathi Appelt

LEARNING ABOUT Expressing Emotions

The hardest thing about preschool for many children is saying goodbye to Mom or Dad each morning. This book offers comforting words and warm illustrations perfect for sharing when little ones in your class are having a hard-to-say-goodbye day.

Help ease the transition from home to preschool by reading this story for read-aloud at the beginning of the new school year. Send a copy home with those children having a particularly difficult time making this transition to encourage a warm discussion between loved ones and little ones.

For a more tangible reminder of this ever-present love, let students make two simple heart necklaces—one for themselves and the other for a loved one. Have them shape small hearts out of clay, make a hole for string, and let dry. After they paint the hearts, add a printed note with the following words from *Oh My Baby, Little One*:

> *Even when I'm far away,*
> *this love I have will stay*
> *and wrap itself around you*
> *every minute of the day.*

Children will feel closer to their loved ones as they keep these reminder pendants around their necks, tucked inside their pockets, their lunch bags, or even their shoes. This symbol of love will be with them the whole day through.

Rich Vocabulary

nestles *v.* snuggles

Pete's a Pizza

by William Steig

Adjusting Feelings

Pete's in a bad mood.
Just when he's supposed to play ball with the guys, it decides to rain.
Pete's father can't help noticing how miserable his son is.
He thinks it might cheer Pete up to be made into a pizza.

— From *Pete's a Pizza*, pages 3–7

> **Rich Vocabulary**
>
> **miserable** *adj.* very unhappy

The story of *Pete's a Pizza* is based on a game author William Steig used to play with his youngest daughter, Maggie. Your preschool children will giggle as Dad stretches, whirls, twirls, oils, and flours Pete before adding tomatoes and cheese. Unlike most pizzas, this one giggles when its dough is tickled and, just as this pizza is about to be sliced, it runs away. Fortunately, the pizza is captured—and hugged.

Set up a pizza-making center for your students. On a rainy day, read *Pete's a Pizza* and then provide bins of items so students can turn each other into pizzas—just like Pete. Use items suggested in the story as pizza toppings (a small container labeled flour, checkers, pieces of paper, and so on) to sprinkle on your preschooler pizzas.

MORE FUN WITH THE BOOK

- Set up a kitchen center where students can shape pizza out of Play Dough and use play cooking utensils, pans, and oven mitts. You can also use craft foam.
- A pizza puzzle may be borrowed from your library or a student. This activity encourages the exploring of equal parts, counting of toppings, and other creative fun.

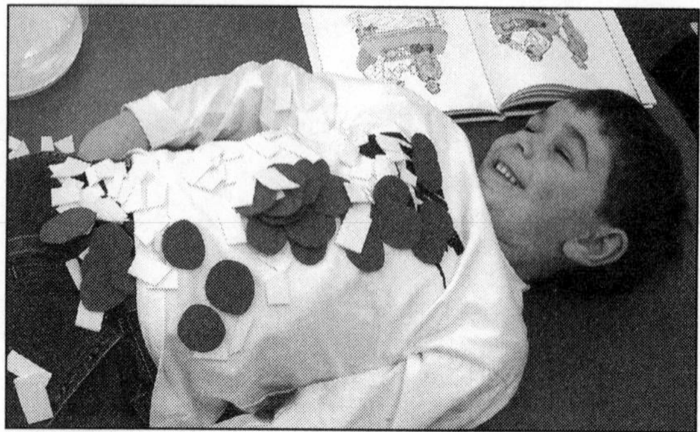

Making pizzas

> **Even More Must-Have Books for Any Kind of Day**
>
> *Chocolate Covered Cookie Tantrum* by Deborah Blumenthal
> *All by Myself* by Aliki
> *Off to School Baby Duck* by Amy Hest
> *Tell Me What It's Like to Be Big* by Joyce Dunbar
> *Oh!* by Kevin Henkes
> *The Cloud Book* by Eric Carle
> *Carl's Afternoon in the Park* by Alexandra Day
> *A Boy, A Dog and a Frog* by Mercer Mayer
> *Little Whistle's Dinner Party* by Cynthia Rylant
> *Grump* by Janet S. Wong
> *A Summery Saturday Morning* by Margaret Mahy

Name ______________________________ Date ____________________

Feelings Wheel

Color and cut out the feelings wheel.

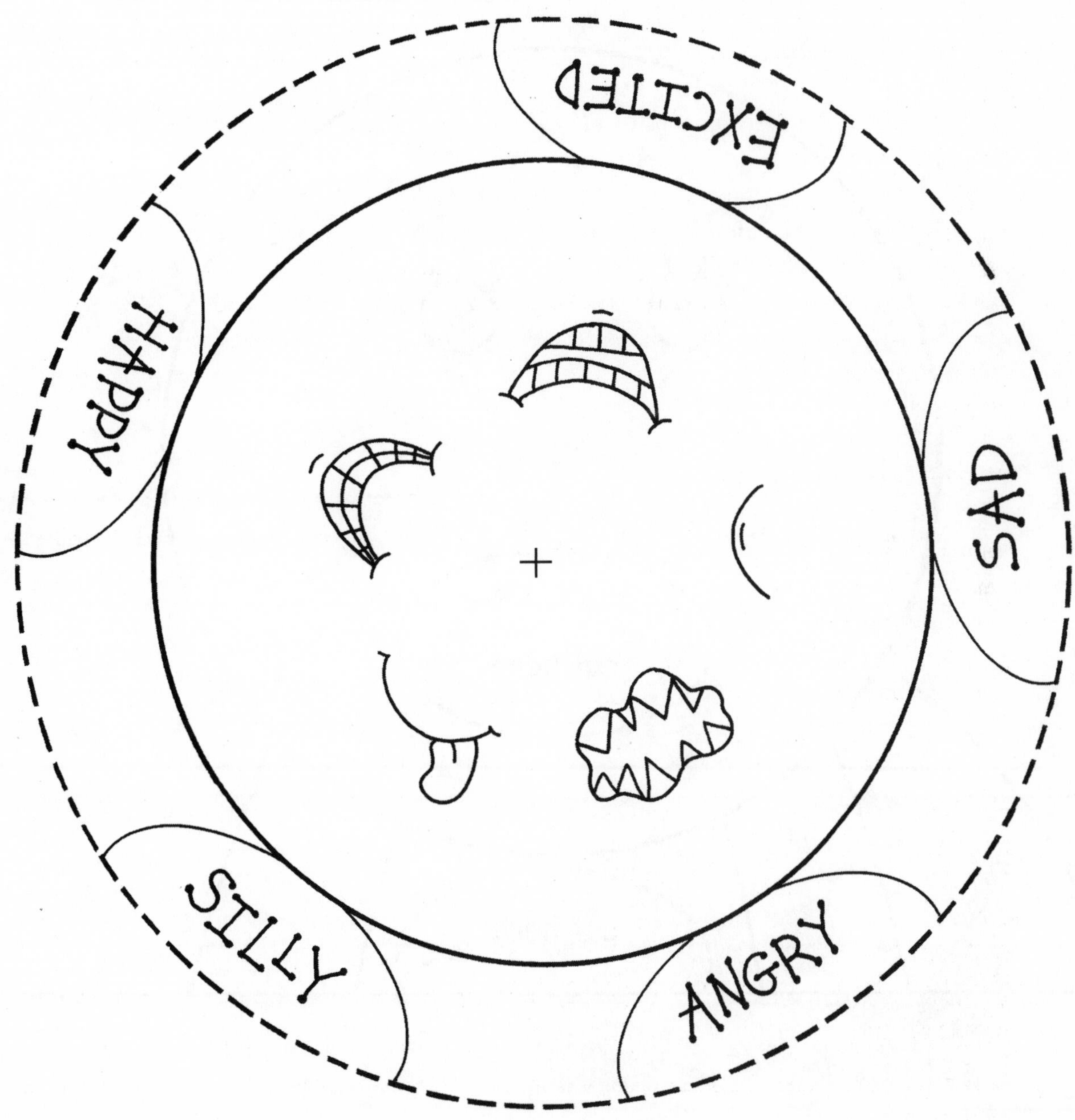

Use with *Today I Feel Silly and Other Moods That Make My Day* by Jamie Lee Curtis.

Name ______________________________ Date ____________________

Today I Feel . . .

Color the face. Cut out the mouth.

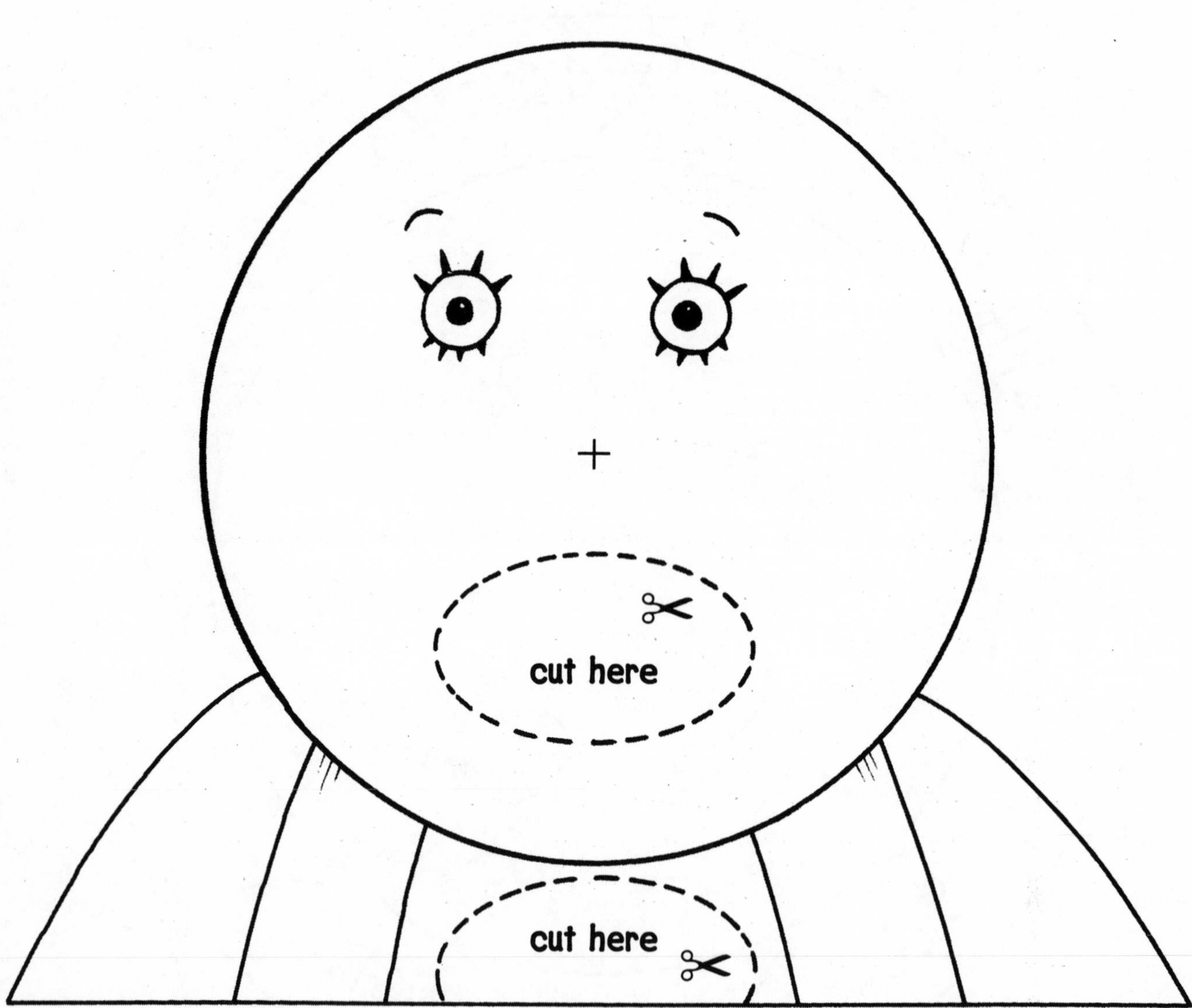

Use with *Today I Feel Silly and Other Moods That Make My Day* by Jamie Lee Curtis.

Name ______________________ Date ______________

My Favorite Things

My favorite animal is ______________________.

My favorite color is ______________________.

My favorite fruit is ______________________.

My favorite food is ______________________.

My favorite toy is ______________________.

My favorite season is ______________________.

My favorite place is ______________________.

My favorite book is ______________________.

Here is a picture of me with one of my favorite things.

Use with *The Everything Book* by Denise Fleming.

Chapter 3: Now I Know My ABC's and 123's

10 Must-Have Alphabet and Counting Books

Chapter Learning Goals:

* identifying letters *A* to *Z*
* identifying letter sounds
* printing letters *A* to *Z*
* identifying numbers 1 to 10
* counting from 1 to 10
* printing numbers 1 to 10
* exploring one-to-one correspondence

Helping young children make sense of the world around them and providing appropriate channels for their incessant curiosity and wonderment make the preschool years perfect for exploring letters and numbers. Identifying letters and numbers in the context of a great book proves their relevance to the real world and, more importantly, provokes the desire to make sense of letters and numbers "so I can read and count all by myself."

Explore the house in *Little Bear's ABC and 123* to look for things that begin with each letter of the alphabet and to count things. Meet the rambunctious letters who challenge one another to race to the top of the coconut tree in *Chicka Chicka Boom Boom*. Feel the letters with the quiet beauty of *The Handmade Alphabet*. Let Miss Spider spin a web of *ABC*'s with the help of her friends. Dr. Seuss takes children on a rhyming alphabet journey that gives examples of things that begin with all the letters from *A* to *Z*.

"Count on" *Fish Eyes* and *The Very Hungry Caterpillar* for tangible die-cut counting pages that are just right for little fingers to touch. Count down to bedtime with *Ten, Nine, Eight*. Denise Fleming's *Count!* presents an array of brightly colored animals from zebras to worms to count and then count again. And finally, count the animals getting off the train in *1,2,3 to the Zoo*.

Enjoy the must-have alphabet and counting books and activities in this chapter for some fun-filled, book-based *ABC*'s and 123's practice.

10 Must-Have Alphabet and Counting Books

Little Bear's ABC and 123 by Jane Hissey

Chicka Chicka Boom Boom by Bill Martin Jr. and John Archambault

The Handmade Alphabet by Laura Rankin

Miss Spider's ABC by David Kirk

Dr. Seuss's ABC by Dr. Seuss

Fish Eyes: A Book You Can Count On by Lois Ehlert

The Very Hungry Caterpillar by Eric Carle

Ten, Nine, Eight by Molly Bang

Count! by Denise Fleming

1,2,3 to the Zoo: A Counting Book by Eric Carle

MINI-LESSON IN ACTION

Little Bear's ABC and 123

by Jane Hissey

Beginning Letter Sounds

A is for animals. All the animals are asleep except Little Bear.
B is for box. Bramwell Brown has a big box of buttons.
C is for cake. Bramwell is cutting a piece for Camel.
— From *Little Bear's ABC and 123*, pages 2–4

Jane Hissey's irresistible band of animal friends—Little Bear, Camel, Hoot, Zebra, Duck, Rabbit, Ruff, Old Bear, and more—are featured in this collection of two stories in one. The soft, warm, and realistic illustrations make the characters come alive and look real enough to be hugged. Each page of "Little Bear's ABC" features a letter from the alphabet. The text includes highlighted examples of words beginning with each letter, and a box highlighting the capital and lower forms appears at the top of each page. Blends such as *th, ch,* and *sh* are also introduced.

Perfect to share with small groups that are concentrating on particular letter sounds, *Little Bear's ABC and 123* also makes a wonderful overall introduction to the alphabet. In the mini-lesson that follows, we have just read the first story, "Little Bear's ABC," and are revisiting Little Bear and his friends to reinforce letter recognition.

Introduce students to Little Bear's friend, Old Bear, and his bag of favorite things. Then have children select objects from a bag and identify the beginning letter sound for each object. To prepare for this mini-lesson, gather a small bag of objects that begin with selected letters of the alphabet, a set of magnetic or other alphabet letters, alphabet strips for each student (see the reproducible on page 57), and a stuffed bear or other animal tucked in a shoe box (see the *Qq* page in "Little Bear's ABC"). Tape the following note to the lid:

> **Rich Vocabulary**
>
> **naughty** *adj.* not behaving

Dear Boys and Girls,
This is my friend, Old Bear. He is a very friendly bear.
Would you please keep him company today? Old Bear wants to help you learn your ABC's. I'm off to the library to find alphabet books to help him. Here is a bag of his favorite things to keep him happy. Thanks for your help!
Love,
Little Bear

The children are gathered around me and their individual alphabet strips are placed on the floor in front of them.

Mrs. L.: When I got to school today, I found this box and note on my desk. Let me read it to you. *(I read aloud the note.)*

Megan: We know lots of letters. Old Bear won't believe it!

Mrs. L.: I agree. Maybe we should start by saying the *ABC*'s while I put our magnetic letters in alphabet order. Touch each letter on your *ABC* line, and say the alphabet with me, please.

Class: *A, B, C, D, E, F, G, H, I, J, K, L, M, N, O, P, Q, R, S, T, U, V, W, X, Y, Z.*

Mrs. L.: Nice work! Point to the letter on your *ABC* line that begins O-O-O-Old Bear's name. I'll give you a hint: My mouth forms this letter when I say his name. *(I make an exaggerated O with my mouth).*

Class: O!

Mrs. L.: Great! His last name is B-B-B-Bear. What letter does *Bear* begin with?

Class: *B*!

Mrs. L.: That's right. Now, who wants to see what's inside Old Bear's bag?

Zachary: I'll pick something. It's a ball.

Mrs. L.: B-B-B-Ball. What letter does ball begin with? Point to the letter on your *ABC* line, please.

Class: *B*.

Mrs. L.: Right! Zachary, would you put the ball on the chalk ledge and place the magnetic *B* above it? Great. Ball begins with the letter *B*. Let's try another one.

Ryan: I'll pick something. It's a truck.

Mrs. L.: T-T-T-Truck.

Class: *T*.

Mrs. L.: Excellent! Find the letter *T* on your *ABC* line. Ryan, will you move the truck and the letter *T*? Truck begins with the letter *T*.

Casey: My turn. This must be Old Bear's cup. That starts with *K*.

Mrs. L.: *K* does make the *k-k-k* sound. But *cup* begins with the other letter that makes the k-k-k sound.

Class: *C*!

Mrs. L.: Right! *C* and *K* both make the *k* sound. With practice, you'll know which words begin with *C* and which words begin with *K*. Casey, please place the cup on the chalk ledge with the letter *C* while the rest of you find *C* on your *ABC* lines.

Michael: I'll look for something else in the bag. It's a little book.

Ben: I know that one. It's *B*—just like my name.

Tommy: And *bear* and *ball*.

Blake: The ball was in the bag.

Mrs. L.: Wow! You're great at things that begin with the letter *B*! Let's see what else Old Bear has in his bag.

Rebecca: There's a blanket in the bag. That's begins with *B*, too.

Mrs. L.: Yes, it does.

Rebecca: I'll cover Old Bear with his blanket.

Mrs. L.: He does look a little sleepy. All this hard work with the *ABC*'s has probably made him tired. Let's check his bag for another favorite thing.

Brittany: I found some paper that has a smiley-face pencil on it.

Mrs. L.: P-P-P-Paper and a p-p-p-p-encil.

Class: *P*!

Michael: Old Bear must like to draw with the pencil on the paper.

Ryan: Or write stories or messages.

Mrs. L.: Let's all take out a finger pencil and make a *P* in the air for paper and pencil. Be sure that your *P* has the loop on the right side. *(We continue the lesson until each object in Old Bear's bag has been selected.)*

ON ANOTHER DAY

Read "Little Bear's 123." Using individual number lines cut from the reproducible on page 58 and counters to represent the items in the story, direct students to count along with the read-aloud. Have them show 1 counter to represent the 1 sock, 2 counters to show 2 shadows, and so on. This activity keeps little fingers occupied while making the story hands-on.

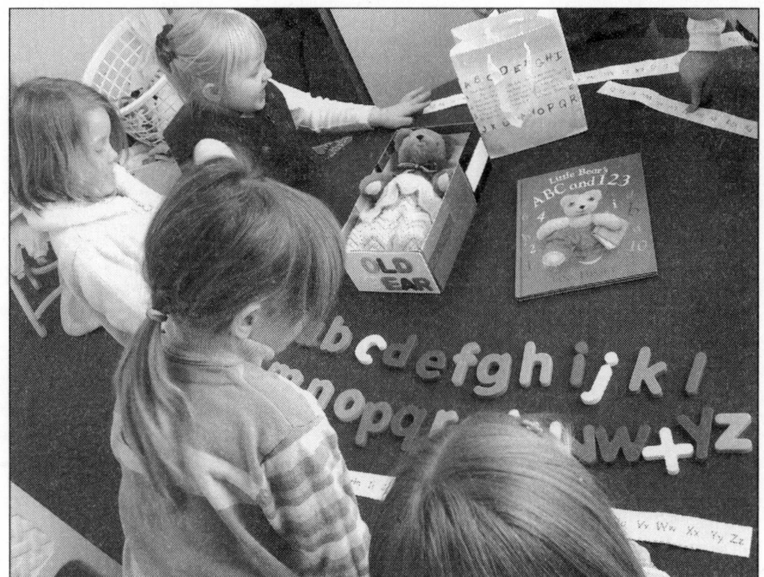

Learning our *ABCs* with Old Bear

More Must-Have Alphabet and Counting Books

Chicka Chicka Boom Boom

by Bill Martin Jr. and John Archambault

Letter Recognition

A *told* ***B****,*
and ***B*** *told* ***C****,*
"I'll meet you at the top
of the coconut tree."

"Whee!" said ***D***
to ***E F G****,*
"I'll beat you to the top
of the coconut tree."

Chicka chicka boom boom!
— From *Chicka Chicka Boom Boom*, pages 5–8

Rich Vocabulary

tangled *v.* twisted around

stooped *v.* bent over

This delightfully bright book with a rollicking beat invites participation from young children. With each turn of the page, another lowercase letters joins the race to the top of the coconut tree. As the letters fill up the tree, the trunk begins to bend until—"Oh, no! Chicka chicka BOOM! BOOM!"

Set up a center based on this must-have book where students can practice identifying lowercase letters in a variety of ways. Arrange baskets of foam or magnetic letters for students to arrange in alphabetical order as they listen to *Chicka Chicka Boom Boom* on audiotape (Scholastic Cassettes, 1989).

Also look for *Chicka Chicka Sticka Sticka*, a sticker version of the book *Chicka Chicka ABC* with reusable letters that "stick-on" the lowercase alphabet in the text. *The Chicka Chicka ABC Magnet Book* is another hands-on version that includes 26 magnetic letters and an easel-back stand perfect for small group demonstrations. A magnetic sheet is moved from page to page so students can match letters as the story is read.

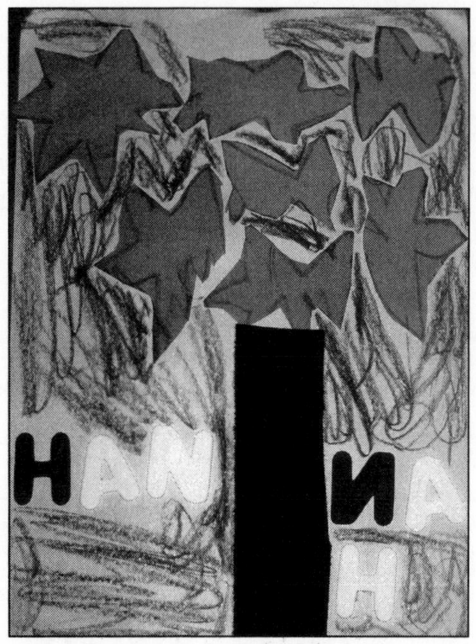

MORE FUN WITH THE BOOK

For a *Chicka Chicka Boom Boom*-based art project, have students draw or cut out a coconut tree and glue it onto white background paper. Provide foam letters and glue so they can add letters that race to the top of the tree.

The Handmade Alphabet

by Laura Rankin

Letter-Sound Relationships

When I first showed this book to my class, one child asked, "Where are the words?" I proceeded to tell him that *The Handmade Alphabet* is a quiet book, just like the world is to someone who is deaf. We talked about the word *deaf* and how deaf people learn a different kind of alphabet—the manual or "handmade" alphabet.

Laura Rankin's book is a beautiful introduction to the manual alphabet. Each page depicts a hand forming a letter of the manual alphabet as it holds an item that begins with that letter sound. On the *A* page, a hand grasps a handful of asparagus, the *B* page has bubbles floating around a hand, a cup dangles from the thumb of the hand shaping the letter *C*, and so on.

As I read each page to the class, we sign the letters and identify the words that begin with each sound. Children love these "hand plays" and are instantly motivated to master each hand shape.

Share this book for read-aloud time, and then place it next to your gathering space. Use it to introduce a letter and sign of the day or week. Once students have committed the manual alphabet to memory, remind them to "take out their 'signs'" when they are saying the alphabet, practicing letter sounds, and spelling simple words. The manual alphabet keeps little fidgeting hands moving productively and gives preschoolers who are learning letter-sound recognition a way of "feeling" each letter.

ON ANOTHER DAY

We make a handmade alphabet of our own. I place individual alphabet letters in a hat, one for each student (for 15 students, I use the first 15 letters of the alphabet). Each student chooses a letter from the hat and then finds an object that begins with that sound. I snap a picture of indi-

Rich Vocabulary

language *n.* the way people speak or write to share ideas with each other

vidual hands forming the letter while holding the object. We do the remaining letters together—one a day until we reach *Z*. We display our handmade alphabet on a bulletin board and refer to it often.

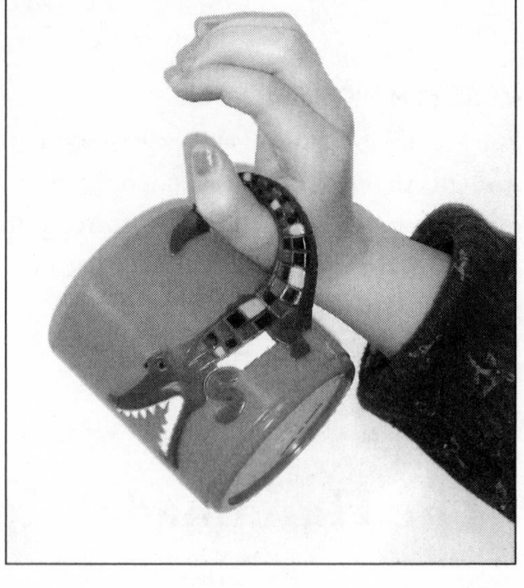

Miss Spider's ABC

by David Kirk

LEARNING ABOUT **Printing Letters**

Ants await.
Bumblebees blow balloons.
Caterpillars circle . . . dragonfly decorations.
— From *Miss Spider's ABC*, pages 2–5

In *Miss Spider's ABC*, David Kirk's buggy friends from *A* to *Z* are back with a surprise for Miss Spider. But don't stop reading at *Z* or you'll miss the most fun of all: The bumblebees blow balloons, the dragonflies decorate, and everyone hides in preparation for Miss Spider's surprise birthday party!

After enjoying the beautiful illustrations and alphabet alliteration, have a little alphabet fun of your own. First, write the alphabet vertically on chart paper, filling in student names from *A* to *Z*. Add words with a birthday theme to create an *ABC* book based on the simple pattern of *Miss Spider's ABC*. Challenge students to work on any difficult letters for "homework." Have them work at the art center to draw pictures of designated tasks from *A* to *Z*. Staple the pages together as a class alphabet book. Each day, give a different student a chance to take the book home to share with parents.

Our ABC Birthday Party
All arrange chairs.
Ben & Blake & Brittany bake birthday cake & blow up balloons.
Casey collects candy & candles.
Decorations
Everyone eats.
Food
Gifts galore!

Rich Vocabulary

entertain *v.* to keep a person busy by doing fun things

Happy birthday hats
Ice cream & icing
Jack & Jared jump for joy.
Kites are flying.
Licking spoons of icing
Megan & Michael make music.
Noisemakers
Open the presents.
Paper plates & presents
Quiet hiding
Rachel, Rebecca, & Ryan run with ribbons.
Shhh! Surprise! Spoons & streamers
Tommy fills treat bags
Under the table.
Victoria's very excited when she finds
Wrapping paper with bugs on it & counts
Xtra pieces of cake.
Yellow balloons
Zachary zooms to the door!

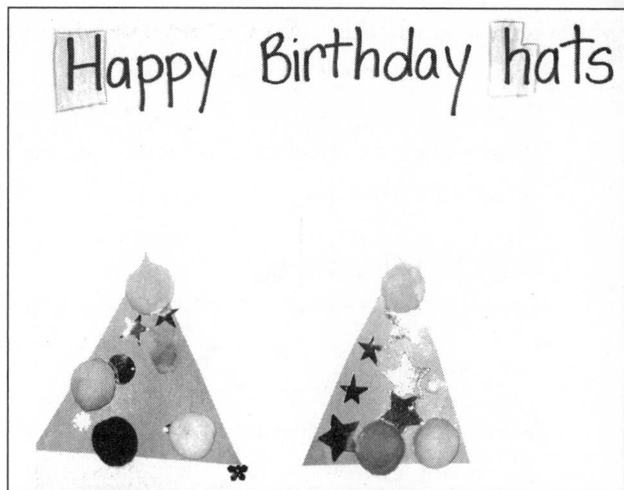

Our H Page: Happy Birthday hats

Dr. Seuss's ABC

by Dr. Seuss

Identifying Letters and Letter-Sound Relationships

BIG A
little a
What begins with A?
Aunt Annie's alligator . . . A . . . a . . . A
— From *Dr. Seuss's ABC*, pages 3–5

What begins with *B*? *C*? *D*? *E*? *F*? *G*? and all the way to *Z*? This rhyming alphabet book by Dr. Seuss is perfect for exploring two skills at once. First, have students arrange letters on a magnetic puzzle with capital and lowercase letters for some matching practice. Then set up a learning center with objects that begin with each letter so students can answer Dr. Seuss's question of "What begins with ________?" for letter-sound

Rich Vocabulary

mumbling *v.* speaking in a low voice that's hard to hear

reinforcement. Although you may not be able to find a Zizzer-Zazzer-Zuzz for *Z* to place in the center, a zipper will do just fine!

For a read-along, read-aloud, challenge students to echo you and repeat the lines of Dr. Seuss's wonderfully wacky, forever classic alphabet book while they gain letter reinforcement at the same time.

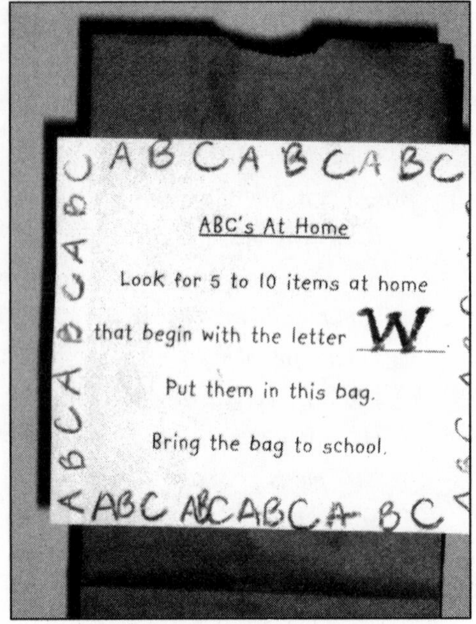

MORE FUN WITH THE BOOK

Make copies of the note below, and staple it onto the front of a small paper bag for each student. Students fill their bags with items from home that begin with the letter sound being studied. The next day during circle time, they share bags, highlighting the beginning letter sound of each item.

> *ABC's at Home*
> *Look for five to ten items at home that begin with the letter W.*
> *Put them in this bag. Bring the bag to school.*

Fish Eyes: A Book You Can Count On

by Lois Ehlert

Counting From 1 to 10

If I could put on a suit of scales,
add some fins and one of these tails,
I'd close my eyes and then I'd wish
that I'd turn into a beautiful fish.
— From *Fish Eyes*, pages 2–5

In this bright, die-cut book, Lois Ehlert has created a feast for readers' eyes while providing hands-on counting practice that's a little fishy. On a bulletin board covered with blue butcher block paper for the sea, attach buttons or paper fasteners to represent fish eyes.

For an extra sweet hands-on read-along read-aloud, pass out packs of Swedish Fish (gummy candy fish available at most grocery stores) for students to use as counters for a little math fun.

> **Rich Vocabulary**
>
> **flashy** *adj.* brightly colored

Display a sheet of blue paper as a water background. Call on volunteers to roll a number cube and then read the number to the class. Students arrange that number of fish on the blue paper, and count them. Reinforce one-to-one correspondence as students point to each fish as they count. End the lesson by having students line up a certain number of fish in the water, eat one, and then count the number of fish that are left. Continue until all the fish have been eaten—children won't complain when they're asked to eat these fish!

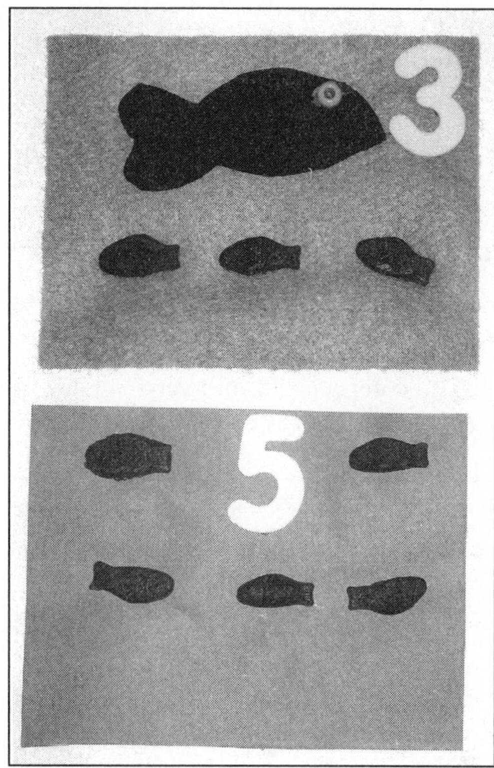

Counting fish

ON ANOTHER DAY

On the last page of the book, the little black fish asks readers: "If you could truly have a wish, would you wish to be a fish?" Set up an art center where students can create the fish they would be—striped, spotted, smiling, green, skinny, fan-tailed, or flashy. Cut various fish shapes out of different colored construction paper for students to choose. Using lick-and-stick paper, paper-punched dots, glue sticks, and scrap shapes, encourage students to create a collage fish using Lois Ehlert's favorite illustrating technique. Hang a sheet of blue butcher block paper for fish to swim on.

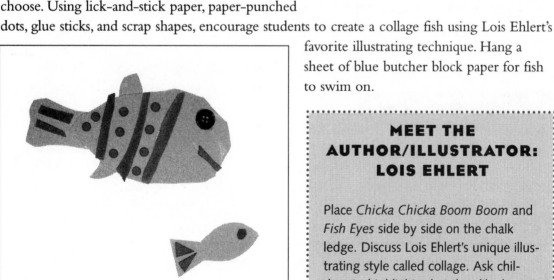

Would you wish to be a fish?

MEET THE AUTHOR/ILLUSTRATOR: LOIS EHLERT

Place *Chicka Chicka Boom Boom* and *Fish Eyes* side by side on the chalk ledge. Discuss Lois Ehlert's unique illustrating style called collage. Ask children to highlight what they like best about her illustrations. Share the video *Color World: A Video Visit with Lois Ehlert* (Harcourt Brace & Company, 1994) to further get to know this favorite author/illustrator. Also set up a reading corner with more great books by Lois Ehlert for children to browse during free time.

The Very Hungry Caterpillar

by Eric Carle

LEARNING ABOUT Printing Numbers From 1 to 10

The cute, colorful, and very hungry caterpillar who munches his way through this great book counts his food and names the days of the week for preschool readers.

On Saturday, he ate through one piece of chocolate cake,
one ice-cream cone, one pickle, one slice of Swiss cheese,
one slice of salami, one lollipop, one piece of cherry pie,
one sausage, one cupcake, and one slice of watermelon.
That night he had a stomachache!

— From *The Very Hungry Caterpillar*, pages 16–17

Rich Vocabulary

nibbled *v.* ate in small bites

I had read this book countless times with my children for it is one of our top ten favorite books. Then one rainy afternoon, after a quick trip to a craft store, I covered our easel with a large piece of black felt and proceeded to cut smaller felt pieces for food and a very hungry caterpillar. As I cut, Ryan and Maddie added details to the fruit with a felt marker, glued on stems, and referred to the book to make sure I had made the appropriate number of each tasty felt treat. When our work was complete, I sat back and said, "Now you can tell the story to me!"

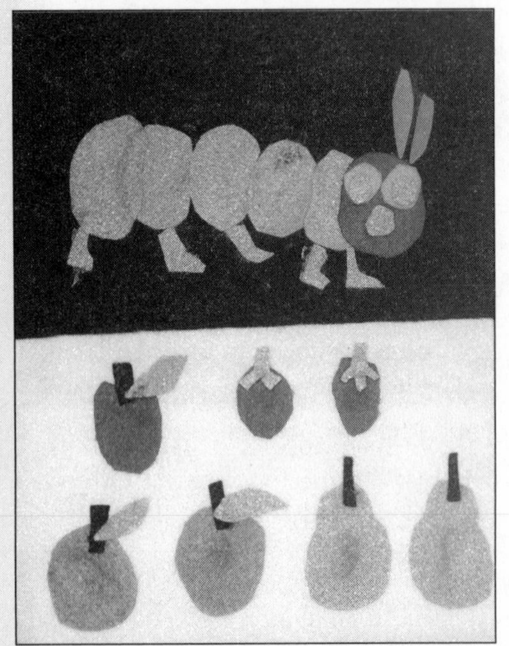

Counting with *The Very Hungry Caterpillar*

This felt board activity brings the book to life and makes read-aloud interactive for preschool children. Enlist the help of parent volunteers to cut out simple fruit shapes from felt or purchase a felt kit of this story. (I discovered such a kit at the library a week after making my own!)

After retelling the story, try a little introduction to printing the numbers from 1 to 10. Begin by placing one of the felt food pieces on the felt board and asking children to count the number of things the very hungry caterpillar eats. Provide individual chalkboards for students so they can practice printing the number 1 as you demonstrate how to write it on chart paper or the board. Continue adding felt objects and recording the numbers from 2 to 10. With all 10 objects displayed on the board, say, "He ate 1, now there are 9." Count back, and record the numbers from 9 to 0.

TEACHING TIP

Using *The Everything Book* in ABC and 123 Learning Centers

Don't let books used in previous chapters sit on your bookshelf for too long. For example, Denise Fleming's *The Everything Book* (see Chapter 2) is perfect for reinforcing alphabet, number, word, and shape recognition as well as graphing. Give the following activities a try:

ABC Practice (pages 22–23) Provide fingerpaint and paper for students to practice writing the alphabet using these pages as a guide. Use bug stamps as a reward for careful work—to replicate Denise Fleming's ladybug flying across the page.

Word Fun (pages 18–19) Display items such as the kitchen toys shown on page 18 along with word cards so students can match each item to the corresponding word. Encourage them to use beginning letter clues to assist with word identification.

Fruit Colors (pages 16–17) The fruit-loving, hungry mouse from Denise Fleming's *Lunch* reappears on page 16 of *The Everything Book* to help reinforce color recognition. Give students an opportunity to practice drawing and coloring the fruit that mouse likes to nibble. Provide word cards with color words so students can practice reading by using beginning letter clues.

Counting Fun (pages 24–25) Fill plastic eggs with 1 to 5 of the same object (dinosaur counters or teddy bear counters work well). Students open each egg, count the objects inside, and then place the eggs in numerical order.

Counting Ladybugs (pages 62–63) There are 119 ladybugs crawling or flying across the pages of *The Everything Book.* Page 62 lists how many ladybugs are on each page. Have students play a game of I Spy the Ladybugs with partners. Place sticky notes marked with specific numbers of ladybugs for students to find: 17 ladybugs on pages 1, 2, and 62 ; 13 ladybugs on pages 3 and 63; 5 ladybugs on page 24; 2 ladybugs on pages 29–31. Explain that pages without sticky notes have just 1 ladybug to find.

Shape Pictures (pages 20–21) Have a parent volunteer cut shapes of various sizes out of different-colored construction paper. Place these shapes, glue sticks, and background paper at a center for students to create shape pictures using the illustration on page 21 as a guide.

Our Pet Graph (page 42–43) After sharing these pages, have students participate in a graphing activity to illustrate the number and kinds of pets your class has. Label a large sheet of butcher block paper with the title, "Our Pet Graph." Include simple animal shapes for each kind of pet. Invite individual students to add a block or glue a construction-paper square next to the pet(s) that live at their house. When the graph is complete, count the number of each kind of pet and talk about the results of the graph.

Ten, Nine, Eight

by Molly Bang

LEARNING ABOUT **Identifying and Ordering Numbers**

From ten small toes all washed and warm, nine soft friends in a quiet room, and all the way down to one big girl all ready for bed, this countdown to dreamland makes readers feel warm, cozy, and perhaps even a bit sleepy! In this Caldecott Honor book, Molly Bang creates a delightfully relaxing story with illustrations worth counting again and again. Read aloud the story, and then invite children to guess the number of things they have to count at bedtime. After they guess, pass out copies of the reproducible on page 59 for them to take home. Explain that they can do a real countdown at bedtime that night—counting toes, friends, windows, shoes, and so on—just like in *Ten, Nine, Eight.*

The next day, after sharing countdown results, introduce a counting center based on this great book. Label ten shoeboxes or gift bags with a number from 1 to 10 and then cover the numbers with a construction-paper flap. Next fill the containers with the corresponding number of objects from 1 to 10, and place tangible numbers (magnetic, foam, or wooden) nearby. Ask students to count the objects and then find the corresponding number. Lift the flap to reveal the correct number so students receive immediate reinforcement for number identification. Finally have them place the containers in reverse "ten, nine, eight" order.

> **Rich Vocabulary**
>
> **pale** *adj.* without much color

Count!

by Denise Fleming

Representing Numbers 1 to 10

In *Count!*, Denise Fleming has created a book of countable animals from wiggling worms and fluttering butterflies to bouncing kangaroos and jumping zebras. The bright illustrations motivate young eyes to practice counting from 1 to 10 and then by tens to 50 before counting all over again. Each page is arranged with the

> **Rich Vocabulary**
>
> **flutter** *v.* to move up or down

featured number in a box; number, animal, and action words; and a corresponding number of illustrations of shapes and animals.

To extend learning based on this book, provide number-shaped sponges, paint, and paper so students can stamp the numbers from 1 to 10. You can also supply animal-shaped sponges for students to stamp up to 10 objects on paper. They may circle the number of objects or stamp the corresponding number. Create a bulletin board of student work by hanging the sponge-painted pictures around letters that spell COUNT!

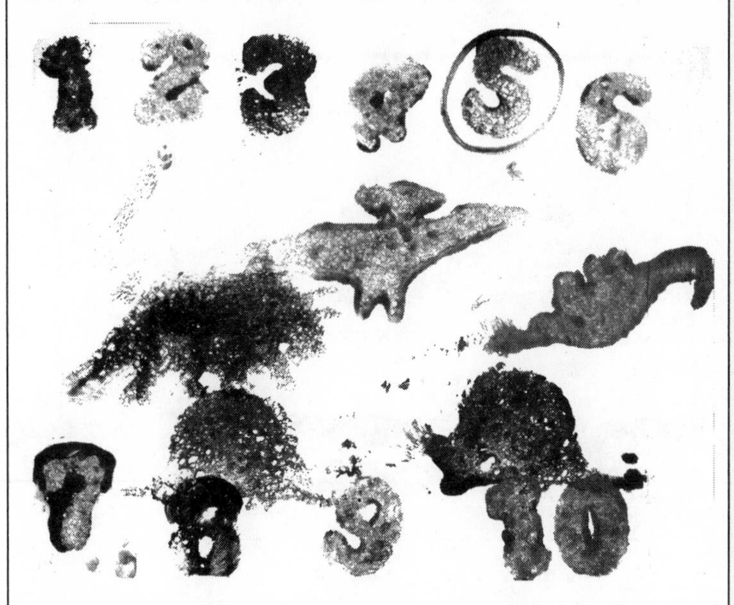

Counting dinosaurs

1,2,3 to the Zoo: A Counting Book

by Eric Carle

LEARNING ABOUT One-to-One Correspondence

Eric Carle's collage animals are riding the train to the zoo. As each page is turned, the next train car of animals is depicted—first 1 elephant, then 2 hippos, 3 giraffes, and so on to 10. A separate, small illustration at the bottom of each page provides additional counting practice as the train grows to include the animals shown on the previous page. The last page folds out to reveal all the animals in their appropriate zoo spaces. The train in the border at the bottom now depicts empty cars. Read the story, count the animals, and then make an animal train of your own using copies of the reproducible on page 60.

Write a number from 1 to 10 on each copy of the reproducible, and then pass out a reproducible to each student. Using pictures of animals cut from magazines or animal stamps or stickers, individuals or small groups of children fill each car with the appropriate number of animals. Display the completed train cars—perhaps with an engine drawn from Eric Carle's example—where students can see their 1,2,3 Zoo and practice counting animals from 1 to 10 over and over again.

Rich Vocabulary

aboard *adv.* on a train, bus, or ship

2 animals going to the zoo

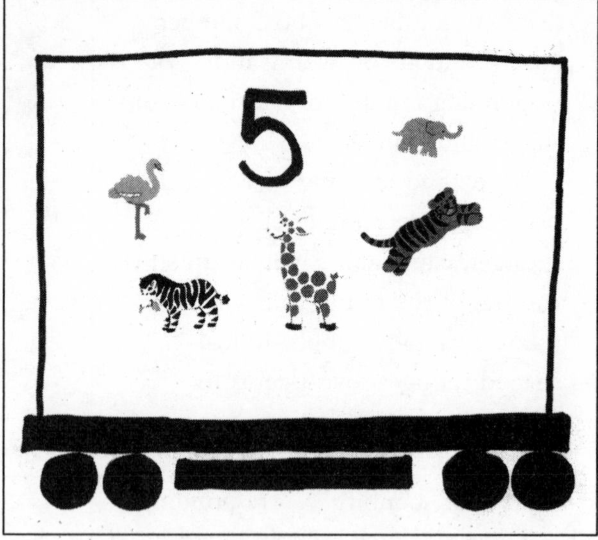

5 animals going to the zoo

Even More Must-Have Alphabet and Counting Books

A My Name Is Alice by Jane Bayer

Alphabears by Kathleen Hague

Alphabet Adventure by Audrey Wood

Mouse Count by Ellen Stoll Walsh

Counting Kisses by Karen Katz

Numbears by Kathleen Hague

Spot Can Count by Eric Hill

Little Rabbit's First Number Book by Alan Baker

Let's Count It Out, Jesse Bear by Nancy White Carlstrom

Counting Crocodiles by Judy Sierra

Alphabets

Teacher Directions: Make one copy for each student. Cut on the dashed lines. Glue the strips side by side to make individual alphabets.

Aa Bb Cc Dd Ee Ff

Gg Hh Ii Jj Kk Ll

Mm Nn Oo Pp Qq

Rr Ss Tt Uu Vv

Ww Xx Yy Zz

Use with *Little Bear's ABC and 123* by Jane Hissey.

Number Lines

Teacher Directions: Cut on the dashed lines to make individual number lines.

1 2 3 4 5 6 7 8 9 10

1 2 3 4 5 6 7 8 9 10

1 2 3 4 5 6 7 8 9 10

1 2 3 4 5 6 7 8 9 10

1 2 3 4 5 6 7 8 9 10

1 2 3 4 5 6 7 8 9 10

1 2 3 4 5 6 7 8 9 10

Use with *Little Bear's ABC and 123* by Jane Hissey.

Name ______________________________ Date ____________________

My Countdown to Dreamland

Write the numbers as you get ready for bed tonight.

10 Count your toes—all washed and warm. ______

9 Count the friends in your quiet room. ______

8 Count the windows or windowpanes in your room. ______

7 Count your shoes. ______

6 Count the books you read before bed. ______

5 Count the buttons on your pajamas or a favorite shirt. ______

4 Count the sleepy eyes in your family. ______

3 Count kisses on cheeks and nose. ______

2 Count the arms that hug you goodnight. ______

1 Count the good times you had today for
sweet dreams tonight. ______

Use with *Ten, Nine, Eight* by Molly Bang.

Name ______________________ Date ______________

Count the Animals Train

What is your number? Put that many animals in the train.

Use with *123 to the Zoo: A Counting Book* by Eric Carle.

Chapter 4: Colors Are All Around Us

10 Must-Have Books About Colors

Chapter Learning Goals:

- recognizing colors
- exploring primary and complementary colors
- matching items of the same color
- sorting objects by color
- identifying color words using beginning letter clues
- identifying and continuing 2-step patterns

Color is appealing to preschoolers; it grabs their attention. Walk down the aisle of any grocery store for proof—purple and green ketchup, multicolored cereal, blue applesauce, and even blue french fries are at eye level for the youngest of shoppers. Think of the vivid colors that dominate the book covers in the children's section of a bookstore versus the more subdued colors on books in areas for older readers. Colorful illustrations motivate children, hold their interest, and enhance their understanding of what is being read on each page. These illustrations, depicting the bright colors all around us, are a child's first adventure into the world of books.

Join the animal characters featured on the pages of the following must-have books as they discover and explore the colors that accentuate the world around them. Explore the colors red, yellow, and blue with three curious mice who dance in *Mouse Paint*. After sharing *Lunch*, make a graph to record children's favorite colors. Encourage children to use colorful words to describe the animals in *Brown Bear, Brown Bear, What Do You See?* Use *Hello, Red Fox* to introduce children to complementary colors. *The Mixed-Up Chameleon* leads to a patterning activity. Work on matching colors with *White Rabbit's Color Book*.

Children will sympathize with the ever-changing chameleon in *A Color of His Own* and learn more about identifying colors. After hearing and seeing *Color Zoo*, children will clamor to make their own colorful zoo. *Planting a Rainbow* will strengthen color identification and sorting skills. Let children's color sense run wild when they dress the turkey in *Blue Hat, Green Hat*.

Grab a few tubs of paint, a box of crayons, some construction paper, and the colorful books featured in this chapter for fun exploration into the world of color.

10 Must-Have Books About Colors

Mouse Paint by Ellen Stoll Walsh
Lunch by Denise Fleming
Brown Bear, Brown Bear, What Do You See? by Bill Martin Jr.
Hello, Red Fox by Eric Carle
The Mixed-Up Chameleon by Eric Carle
White Rabbit's Color Book by Alan Baker
A Color of His Own by Leo Lionni
Color Zoo by Lois Ehlert
Planting a Rainbow by Lois Ehlert
Blue Hat, Green Hat by Sandra Boynton

Mouse Paint

by Ellen Stoll Walsh

LEARNING ABOUT Recognizing Colors

Once there were three white mice on a white piece of paper.
The cat couldn't find them. One day, while the cat was asleep,
the mice saw three jars of paint—one red, one yellow, and one blue.
They thought it was Mouse Paint. They climbed right in . . .
— From *Mouse Paint*, pages 4–8

As the mice step into the different jars of paint, drip puddles on the floor, and dance around, their feet turn into more than the three colors, as if by magic. After a quick dip in the cat's water bowl, they're white once again. Dazzle your preschoolers with a similar experiment. After sharing *Mouse Paint* for read-aloud, provide students with a bit of color identification and exploration, and matching practice based on this great book.

Set up a demonstration table with three small jars of paint—red, yellow, and blue—six paintbrushes, six mice cut-outs, and sticky-tack. Display a large piece of white paper. (I put the paper on an easel.) To make the lesson even more interactive, set out scraps of red, yellow, blue, orange, green, and purple construction paper in small paint "jars" to distribute among students. Don't forget to set out a "cat bowl" filled with water to dip the brushes in when students are finished. (An empty plastic margarine tub with *C-A-T* written on it will work just fine). Finally, place large sheets of butcher block paper on a table to serve as a "drop cloth."

Gather your "little mice" quietly around the demonstra-

Rich Vocabulary

exploring *v.* looking at something to learn more about it

tion area—so you won't wake the napping cat—for a fun lesson that reinforces color identification based on the three curious, color-savvy mice from *Mouse Paint.*

Mrs. L.: *(I begin the lesson in a whisper.)* You are very quiet mice. I like the way you tiptoed so quietly to the table. When the cat wakes up from his catnap, I'm sure he'll be hungry for a mouse snack! Before he does, let's do a little *Mouse Paint* experiment. As I reread the story, you can help me mix the colors.

Rachel: Are we going to make purple? That's my favorite.

Mrs. L.: Let's start reading to find out: "Once there were three white mice on a white piece of paper. The cat couldn't find them." Help me put three white mice on our white sheet of paper, please.

Zach: So the cat can't eat them!

Mrs. L.: Exactly. Zach, how about hanging the first mouse? We'll use this sticky-tack so we can get them back down again. Good job, Zach. Now choose someone to place our second mouse on the chart.

Zach: Jack can do it.

Mrs. L.: *(After the three mice have been hung, I continue to read.)* Let's keep reading: "One day, while the cat was asleep, the mice saw three jars of paint—one red, one yellow, and one blue. They thought it was Mouse Paint."

Ryan: We have those same colors of paint on the table.

Mrs. L.: Right. Let's put them in red, yellow, blue order.

Ryan: I'll do it.

Mrs. L.: Thanks. Now we can keep reading: "They climbed right in. Then one was red, one was yellow, and one was blue." I think we should paint one of our mice red, one yellow, and one blue.

Ben: I'll do red.

Mrs. L.: I'll take the first mouse down and put him on the paper drop cloth I've placed on the table.

Tommy: That's what real painters use when they paint.

Mrs. L.: The drips go on the cloth, not on the floor or table and chairs. Ben, do a few quick red strokes to fill in the first mouse. Casey, would you paint the second mouse yellow? Michael, would you make the third mouse blue?

Rachel: Nice painting!

Mrs. L.: I agree. Before the mice dry, we'd better keep reading: "They dripped puddles of paint onto the paper. The puddles looked like fun. The red mouse stepped into a yellow puddle and did a little dance." What color will red mouse make when he steps into the yellow puddle?

Tommy: Green?

Jack & Ryan: No, orange.

Mrs. L.: Let's find out. Victoria, please dip a paintbrush in the yellow puddle (or jar) and paint over the red mouse's feet, mixing the red and yellow together.

Class: It's orange!

Mrs. L.: "'Look,' he cried. 'Red feet in a yellow puddle make orange!' The yellow mouse hopped into the blue puddle. His feet mixed and stirred and stirred and mixed until"—

Tommy: His feet will turn green!

Mrs. L.: Tommy, why don't you paint the yellow mouse's feet blue?

Class: It is green!

Mrs. L.: "'Look down,' said the red mouse and the blue mouse. 'Yellow feet in a blue puddle make green.' Then the blue mouse jumped into a red puddle. He splashed and mixed and danced until"—

Rachel: It's going to make purple!

Mrs. L.: Rachel, would you like to paint the blue mouse's feet red for us?

Class: Purple!

Mrs. L.: "'Purple!' they all shouted. 'Blue feet in a red puddle make purple!' But the paint on their fur got sticky and stiff. So they washed themselves down to a nice soft white and painted the paper instead." I think we should hang our mice up with the new colors we made. We can wash our brushes in the cat's bowl and then paint the paper with each different color in *Mouse Paint*.

Ryan: I'll wash the brushes for you.

Mrs. L.: Thanks! If you haven't had a chance to paint yet, you'll get a chance to as I read the rest of the story. *(We continue to read, pausing to have individuals paint the colors named in the story.)*

ON ANOTHER DAY

Give students a chance to mix Mouse Paints of their own. Provide mice (enlarged from the sample); paintbrushes; and red, yellow, and blue paint so pairs can combine the colors to turn the mice orange, green, and purple.

Our *Mouse Paint* fun continues when I hang a chart with color words on it. Using beginning letter clues, the students match colored mice next to the corresponding color words. The completed chart hangs in our classroom for handy reference when completing fill-in-the-blank color pages—a favorite activity of preschoolers who enjoy honing their staying-in-the-lines technique.

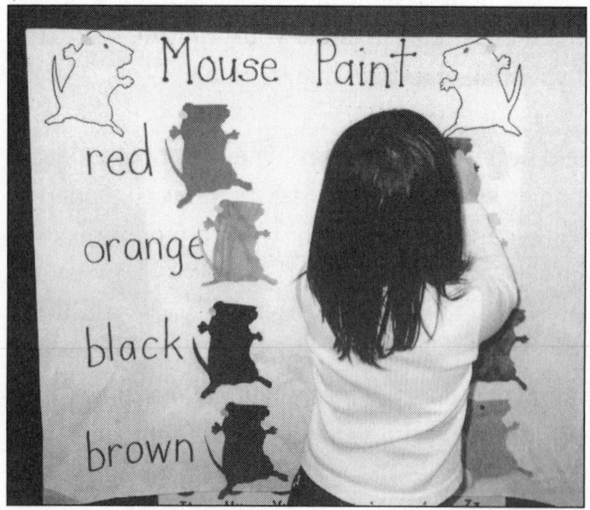

Identifying color words with mouse

Sample mouse

TEACHING TIP

A Color of the Week

My daughter Maddie used to have difficulty identifying names for colors. When asked the color of an object, her answer was always, "Purple?" One day, when I was at my wits' end, I decided to take colors one at a time with her. We identified a color of the week in honor of Maddie, beginning with red. I dressed her from head to toe in red and took her picture, made a Red Book, and even served red candy with red juice. The whole family was aware of the color of the week and acted accordingly. Ryan took his sister on a treasure hunt to collect everything in the house that was red, my husband served Maddie breakfast in her red bowl, and we even ended the week by taking her to the toy store to buy something red. The result? Maddie knows her colors, but purple is still her favorite!

Kick off this chapter of must-have books about the colors around us by designating a color of the week. Adapt the schedule of activities outlined below to suit your needs. Include the great books from this chapter to highlight and emphasize each color of the week.

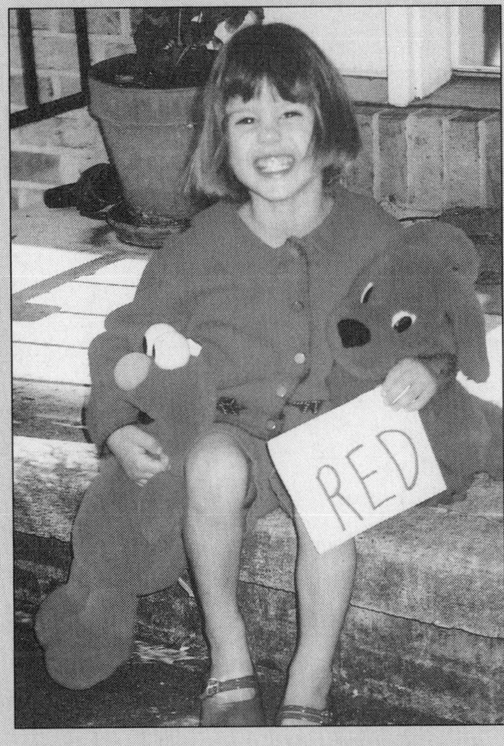

Maddie during "Red Week" with red friends Clifford and Elmo

Plans for Color Week: RED
Monday: Dress in red. Go on a red treasure hunt.
Tuesday: Make a red page for a book of colors.
Wednesday: Eat cookies with red sprinkles for a snack.
Thursday: Sort objects by color—blocks, tub of letters, crayons, and so on.
Friday (Assessment): Find three red items in the room. Select a red prize.

More Must-Have Books About Colors

Lunch

by Denise Fleming

LEARNING ABOUT **Identifying and Graphing Favorite Colors**

Mouse was very hungry.
He was so hungry, he ate a crisp white—
turnip,
tasty orange—
carrots,
sweet yellow—
corn . . .

— From *Lunch*, pages 2–10

And MORE! As Denise Fleming's mouse eats his way through *Lunch*, students get a little yummy color reinforcement. Have them identify their favorite color from this great book about a tasty and oh so colorful lunch enjoyed by one hungry mouse.

After reading aloud the book, throw a Color Tasting Party. Make a picture graph titled "Our Favorite Color to Munch for Lunch." Offer small samples of a few of mouse's lunch foods. For our graphing lesson, I set out orange carrot sticks, frozen green peas (thawed), purple grapes, and red apple slices. After testing a bite of each, children marked the favorite color they tasted with "bites" of construction paper. Purple grapes were the favored taste in our class with red apples coming in close behind!

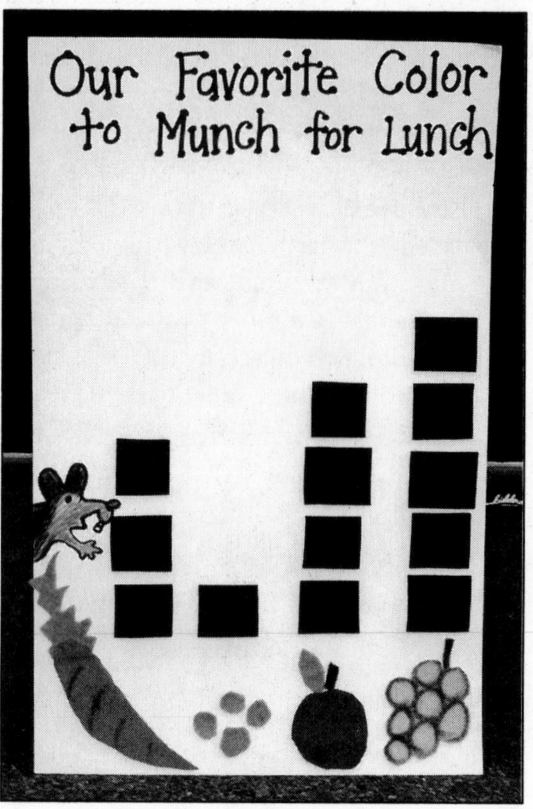

Purple is our favorite color to munch for lunch.

Rich Vocabulary

tasty *adj.* tasting good

tender *adj.* not tough (tender peas)

Brown Bear, Brown Bear, What Do You See?

by Bill Martin Jr.

LEARNING ABOUT Recognizing Colors

Brown Bear, Brown Bear, what do you see?
I see a red bird looking at me.
Red Bird, Red Bird, What do you see?
I see a yellow duck looking at me.
— From *Brown Bear, Brown Bear, What Do You See?*, pages 3–6

> **Rich Vocabulary**
>
> **question** *n.* asking something

This classic great book is just right for teaching voice inflection when reading aloud. Once the simple pattern is identified, students can practice "reading" the story with expression, following the beat, and identifying the colors of each animal.

Duplicate a copy of the glasses frame and mini-book on page 75 for each student. Follow the instructions below to make the glasses and book. You may want to have students help you with some of the steps.

To Make the Glasses:

- *Fold an 8 1/2-inch by 11-inch sheet of oaktag in half.*
- *Place the nosepiece of the glasses on the fold. (See arrow.)*
- *Cut around outline of glasses. Cut out center lens circle.*
- *Tape squares of colored cellophane to the back of each lens. (Use a variety of colors.)*

To Make the Book:

- *Cut out the animal boxes.*
- *Staple the boxes together to make a book.*

Students don their glasses and read their mini-Brown Bear books, retelling the story to match the color they see through their glasses. For example, those wearing green glasses would see a green bear, a green dog, a green cat, and so on. Children may trade glasses for different colored retellings and additional color recognition practice.

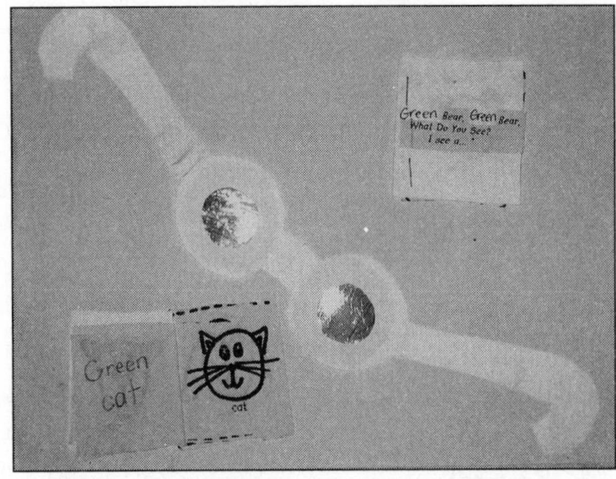

Wearing a pair of green glasses, I see a green cat looking at me.

Hello, Red Fox

by Eric Carle

Exploring Complementary Colors

As I was reading this book to my son Ryan one evening before bed, he tried desperately to see the red fox but continually exclaimed "He's still green, Mommy." Then my husband walked into the room wearing a white shirt. Ryan looked up at him and yelled, "There's the red fox! He's on your shirt, Daddy!"

Eric Carle's play on complementary, or opposite, colors is done simply and uniquely. As Little Frog greets friends arriving for his birthday, his mother questions his understanding of color.

> *"Hello, Red Fox," said Little Frog. "Welcome to my birthday party."*
> *"Thank you for inviting me, " said Red Fox.*
> *"But this is not a red fox," said Mama Frog. "This is a green fox."*
> *"Oh, Mama, you have not looked at the fox long enough," said Little Frog.*
> *Mama Frog looked and looked at the fox or a long time . . .*
> *and, indeed, Little Frog was right!*
>
> — From *Hello, Red Fox*, pages 10–11

In a note at the beginning of *Hello, Red Fox*, Eric Carle explains that Goethe's color theory happened quite similarly. Over 200 years ago, Johann Wolfgang von Goethe was sitting in a tavern, watching a waitress in a red dress. As she moved away, Goethe continued staring at the white wall behind her, and the dress reappeared on the wall in green. Thus began over 20 years of Goethe's research into complementary colors to discover why the dress appeared in green, not red.

Share Carle's important note that describes how to enjoy this book, and then practice with a sample red heart. As students slide their line of vision from the black dot in the center of the red heart across to the black dot on the opposing blank page, slowly count to three, and ask them to watch a green heart appear.

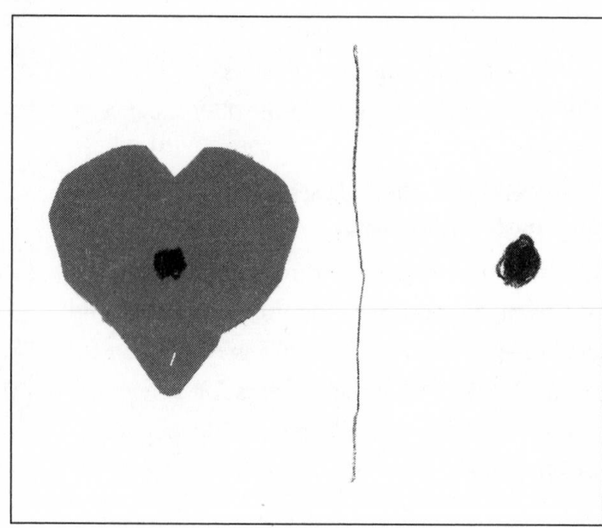

Rich Vocabulary

invite *v.* to ask a person to do something special

Although getting preschool children to focus on the black dot at the center of each animal in this book is challenging, I've found that everyone does eventually see the complementary colors. Having them rest their eyes between attempts and reminding them to do so "quietly and peacefully" as Eric Carle suggests makes for a more relaxing and effective read-aloud time.

Keep this book available for independent perusing, and then make Happy Birthday, Little Frog cards like the one shown. Display pages 20 and 21 of *Hello, Red Fox*, and invite students to cut out a flower for Little Frog's birthday. (You may wish to provide patterns for tracing.) Staple two squares of white paper together to create a card for each student. On the front of the card, write the words *Happy Birthday, Little Frog*. Direct students to cut out a flower or a heart out of construction paper and paste it inside the first (left-hand) page. Then they make a small black dot in the center of the shape. In the center of the opposing blank page, have students make another black dot.

They will enjoy sharing their birthday cards and explaining the complementary color "trick" with members of their family.

Happy Birthday, Little Frog

The Mixed-Up Chameleon

by Eric Carle

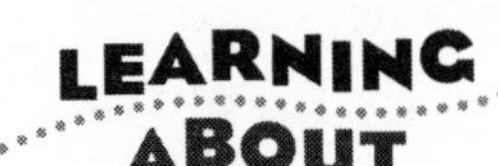

Identifying Color Patterns

The mixed-up chameleon wants to be like the animals in the zoo—handsome like a flamingo, strong like an elephant, funny like a seal, and smart like a fox. When his wishes come true, he is all of these things—and more—at the same time. So when a fly flies past, the very hungry and very mixed-up chameleon is too mixed up to catch it. Only then does the chameleon wish the best wish of all—to be himself.

Talk about how we all feel mixed up at times and wish to have something we don't or to be something we're not. Discuss what it means to be yourself. We can admire the qualities of others—the things that make each of us special—but we'll be happiest when we are being ourselves, just like the mixed-up chameleon.

Then let the colorful chameleon help with an introduction to patterns.

> **Rich Vocabulary**
>
> **sparkling** *adj.* shiny
>
> **dull** *adj.* not shiny

Tape a face and a tongue to a block and introduce it as your mixed-up chameleon. Add body segments, using blocks in a 2-step color pattern for students to continue. Try a few more patterns together, and then invite students to make their own 2-step color-patterned chameleon using tubs of different blocks. (Lego and Duplo blocks work well for this.)

ON ANOTHER DAY

As a follow-up activity, distribute photo faces (made from copies of school photos) for students to glue onto copies of the reproducible on page 76. Have them color the parts to make a Mixed-Up Me page in honor of *The Mixed-Up Chameleon.* Put the pages together to make a class book of patterned chameleons where students identify classmates' patterns.

White Rabbit's Color Book

by Alan Barker

LEARNING ABOUT Recognizing Matching Colors

Exploring the magic of color continues in *White Rabbit's Color Book.* Similar in theme to *Mouse Paint,* this book depicts a lone white rabbit whose curiosity gets the best of her as she dips herself in icy cold blue, sizzling hot red, royal purple, and sunshine yellow. Her final discovery is that blue, yellow, and red mixed together make a lovely warm brown that is just right for her.

For extra color practice, pretend to spill drops of paint from tubs like the ones shown dripping on the back cover of the book. Use a small paint tub with paper scraps to represent different colored paint drops. Accidentally spill the paint drops on the floor, and ask children to clean the floor by picking up the scraps. Then have them match the colors to objects in the room. Ask children to put the paint back into the tub. Spill the paint again and again to reinforce color recognition and matching.

Rich Vocabulary

sizzling *adj.* very hot

A Color of His Own

by Leo Lionni

LEARNING ABOUT Recognizing Colors

Parrots are green
goldfish are red
elephants are gray
pigs are pink.
All animals have a color of their own—
except for chameleons.
They change color wherever they go.

— From *A Color of His Own*, pages 2–7

Rich Vocabulary

remained *v.* stayed

cheerfully *adv.* happily

Leo Lionni writes of a chameleon longing for a color to call his own. He meets an older and wiser chameleon who gently explains that they will never have a color of their own like pigs have pink and elephants have gray. But, he suggests, if they stay side by side, the two of them will always be the same color. They do and live happily ever after being brown together, green together, purple together, and even red-with-white-polka-dots together.

Talk with children about what really made the chameleon live happily ever after. Did having a color of his own, a true friend of his own, or learning to accept himself for who he was really make him happy? Make associations with colors from the book such as pig pink, elephant gray, and parrot green, and then add a few of your own like fire truck red, moon white, and teddy bear brown. Things with a color of their own make color recognition meaningful when it is associated with items from a preschoolers' world.

Brittany's pink collage

Following your discussion, let children find a color of their own with a color-recognition activity. Send them to a work space with a sheet of white paper and one crayon. Have them use the crayon and pictures cut from magazines to make color collages to help Leo Lionni's chameleon see that nothing truly has a color of its own. Complete the activity by attaching a chameleon cut from matching construction paper to blend into each collage color. Display the color collages on A Color of His Own bulletin board.

Color Zoo

by Lois Ehlert

LEARNING ABOUT Exploring Colors and Shapes

Shapes and colors in your zoo, lots of things that you can do.
Heads and ears, beaks and snouts, that's what animals are all about.
I know animals and you do too; make some new ones for your zoo.
— From *Color Zoo*, page 5

In this Caldecott Honor Book, readers visit the color zoo where they can learn to identify the shapes and colors of the animals in this zoo without bars. Three main die-cut shapes are layered to create different animals. As each page is turned, a new animal appears: a tiger made from a circle becomes a mouse from a square and then a fox from a triangle. Each animal is identified on the front of the page and the shape is identified on the back.

Read aloud the book, pointing out the shapes and how one shape removed from each page creates the next animal face. Then identify the colors used to make the animals boldly come alive. Display color words printed on index cards, and ask students to use beginning letter clues to identify the colors that make up each animal.

Set up a center where students can explore shape faces and make new animals for a color zoo of their own. Have parent volunteers make oak-tag patterns for tracing; provide sample animal faces as shown on the last page of *Color Zoo*. Direct students to trace, cut out, and paste shapes onto background paper for bold animal faces. As they identify the colors and shapes they used to create their animals, record these color words on the different shape faces. Display animals in an area labeled "Our Color Zoo."

Our *Color Zoo* mouse

Rich Vocabulary

identify *v.* to name something

Planting a Rainbow

by Lois Ehlert

Sorting By Color

Every year Mom and I plant a rainbow.
In the fall we buy some bulbs and plant them in the ground.
We order seeds from catalogs and wait all winter long
for spring to warm the soil and sprout the bulbs.

— From *Planting a Rainbow*, pages 1–6

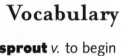

Rich Vocabulary

sprout *v.* to begin to grow

If you think of the books that Lois Ehlert writes as mini-autobiographies, you see how her parents encouraged her creativity and helped her develop the sense of color that has made her books so popular. Ehlert's childhood memory of planting a rainbow with her mother certainly left a bright impression on her, as evidenced in the bold colors found in nature and recreated in this colorful book. As the rainbow grows and grows and grows, the flowers bloom according to the colors highlighted by color tabs. Each flower is also labeled for young plant lovers to identify.

Use this book to stimulate creativity and color appreciation by planting a rainbow in your classroom. Provide different colors of scrap paper, and have students design and cut out flower shapes like those illustrated by Lois Ehlert in *Planting a Rainbow*. Glue the shapes onto Popsicle sticks that have been painted green. Turn small paper cups upside down, and make slits for the craft-stick flower stems. Encourage your young illustrators to include blooms of many colors. Then ask students to sort the flowers by color, and display the creations by color around the room.

MORE ABOUT LOIS EHLERT

At a children's literature conference one spring, I listened to Lois Ehlert describe a table in the corner of her childhood family room. The table was filled with all kinds of wonderful fabric and paper scraps, different kinds of paper, glue, tape, scissors, and various other items about to be discarded. She talked about the fact that because this space was in the central area of the house, not in her room or the basement, her creations were given merit and importance; her earliest work was respected. From this table, Lois Ehlert created her first works of collage.

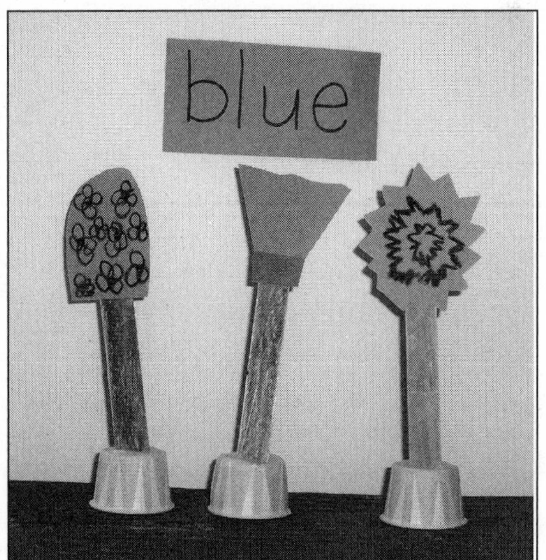

A group of blue flowers

Blue Hat, Green Hat

by Sandra Boynton

Recognizing Color Words

> **Rich Vocabulary**
>
> **ridiculous** *adj.* when something is so silly it makes you laugh

When I picked up Ryan from preschool one morning, he anxiously explained that he borrowed a book to bring home to read to me. "It's the turkey book, Mommy. It is soooo funny. I'm going to make you and Daddy and Maddie laugh, too."

Always in need of a laugh, we sat down together on the couch as soon as we got home, and Ryan proceeded to read *Blue Hat, Green Hat* to Maddie and me. It's true that I did get a laugh at the turkey who doesn't quite know how to dress himself. But more than that, I was impressed by Ryan's enthusiasm for sharing a favorite book with us.

After at least ten rereadings that day, I encouraged Ryan to point to each word as he read the story aloud. He gave this a try until his sister came downstairs with her shirt on upside down. "Just like the turkey," she said. As the two of them giggled around the house, putting hats on their feet, socks on their hands, coats on backwards, and shoes on their heads, there was some serious book-based silliness going on. Dressing my little "turkeys" had never been so much fun!

The next day, I made some paper turkey dolls for Ryan's class to dress and label. Miss Christy reread the crazy story *Blue Hat, Green Hat* to get her preschoolers laughing and identifying colors, and then they dressed turkeys of their own.

For your own *Blue Hat, Green Hat* book-based silliness, and to reinforce color recognition and color word identification, provide students with a copy of the undressed turkey and his clothes on page 77. Have children color and cut out the turkey and clothes. They can label or dictate color words beside each item of "turkey dressing."

Turkey dressing

> **Even More Must-Have Books About Colors**
>
> *Dog's Colorful Day: A Messy Story about Counting and Colors* by Emma Dodd
>
> *Color Farm* by Lois Ehlert
>
> *What Makes a Rainbow?* by Betty Ann Schwartz
>
> *A Rainbow All Around Me* by Sandra L. Pinkney

Name ______________________ Date ______________

What Do You See?

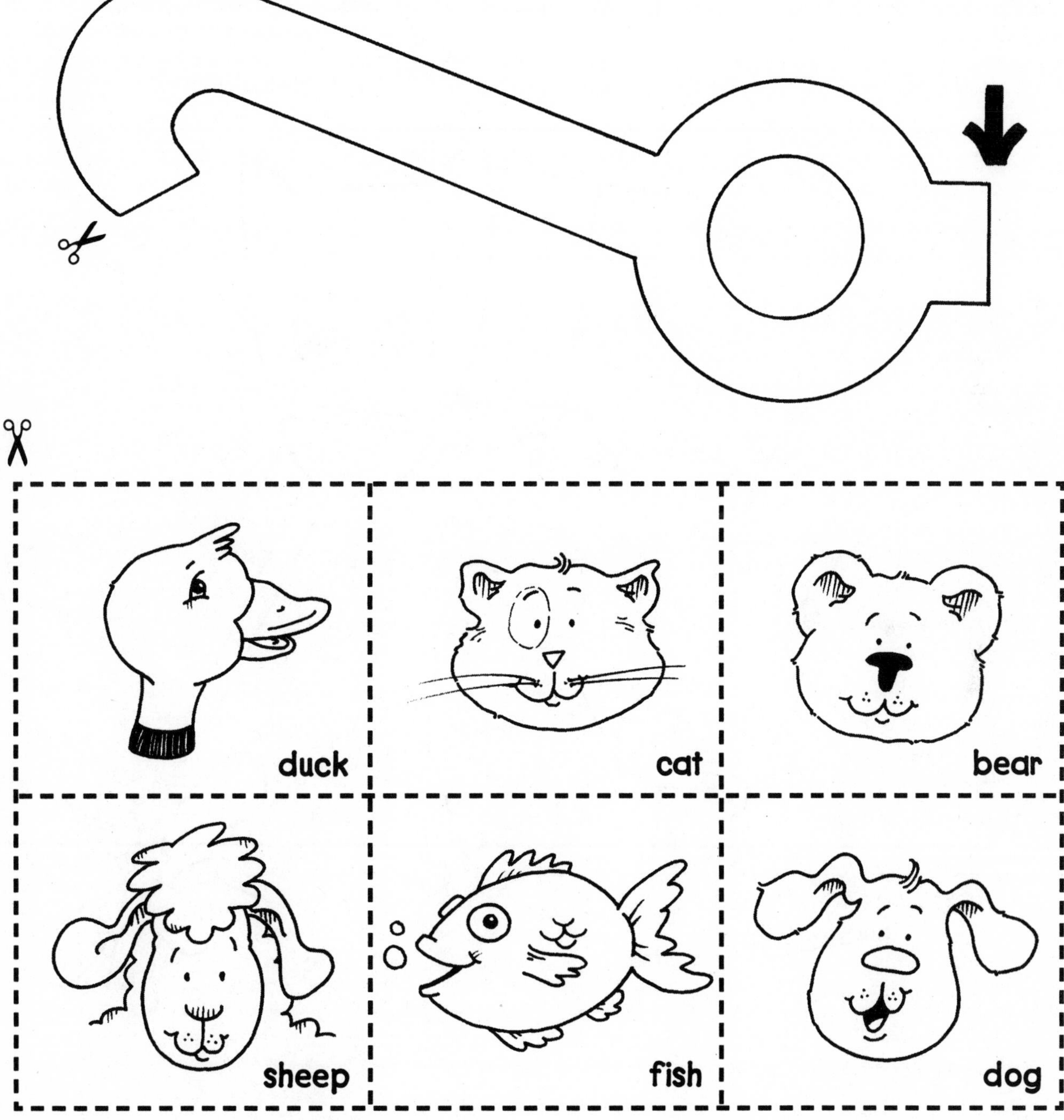

Use with *Brown Bear, Brown Bear, What Do You See?* by Bill Martin, Jr.

Name ______________________________ Date ______________________

Mixed-Up Me

Glue your face below. Color the chameleon's body. Use a 2-step pattern.

Use with *The Mixed-Up Chameleon* by Eric Carle.

Name ________________________________ Date ______________________

Turkey Dressing

Color and cut out the turkey's clothes. Dress the turkey. Write the color words.

Use with *Blue Hat, Green Hat* by Sandra Boynton.

Chapter 5: Time to Sleep

10 Must-Have Bedtime Books

Chapter Learning Goals:

- reading at school and at home every day
- strengthening school-home connections by sharing great books and book-based activities for parents to enjoy with children
- identifying favorite books
- responding to books using creative play, role-playing, and writing
- identifying and exploring the five senses
- strengthening oral language skills
- reinforcing listening skills

There are so many great books written about bedtime that are perfect for sharing with the preschool set. And although sleeping isn't at the top of preschoolers' lists of favorite things to do, teachers of this age group know the importance of providing a time for unwinding and recharging small minds and bodies. Sharing a restful book with a bedtime theme can provide this necessary time for rejuvenation.

But the most important reason for including these great books about bedtime is to encourage reading at home on a daily basis. This chapter is filled with fun ways for parents to make books a part of the bedtime routine. Those new to bedtime books will discover a wonderfully relaxing way to end each day. Parents for whom books have been a part of bedtime will find great book recommendations and activities to enjoy with their children. Introduce the following books and activities to kick off a reading at home incentive program highlighted in this chapter.

Read *Time to Sleep* to explore the five senses. Put the pattern in *Goodnight Moon* to good use in your classroom. Let children design a new set of pj's to celebrate *Pajama Time*. After reading *Kiss Good Night*, encourage students to list four steps in their own bedtime routines.

Barnyard Lullaby and *Time for Bed* lend themselves to activities reinforcing listening skills. Use *How Do Dinosaurs Say Goodnight?* to explore vocabulary and role-playing. In conjunction with *Guess How Much I Love You*, have children express their love for someone. They can help Willa from *Tell Me Something Happy Before I Go to Sleep* by listing happy things. End a read-aloud of *Flora's Blanket* by sending children on a hunt for a hidden blanket.

10 Must-Have Bedtime Books

Time to Sleep by Denise Fleming
Goodnight Moon by Margaret Wise Brown
Pajama Time by Sandra Boynton
Kiss Good Night by Amy Hest
Barnyard Lullaby by Frank Asch
Time for Bed by Mem Fox
How Do Dinosaurs Say Goodnight? by Jane Yolen
Guess How Much I Love You by Sam McBratney
Tell Me Something Happy Before I Go to Sleep by Joyce Dunbar
Flora's Blanket by Debi Gliori

Time to Sleep

by Denise Fleming

LEARNING ABOUT Identifying The Senses

Bear sniffed once.
She sniffed twice.
"I smell winter in the air," said Bear.
"It is time to crawl into my cave and sleep.
But first I must tell Snail."
— From *Time to Sleep*, page 3

Bear and her friends know there is no ignoring the seasonal signs that forecast their upcoming winter nap. Bear smells winter, Snail and Skunk see it in the form of frost and colored leaves. Turtle's proof comes in the fact that the days are growing shorter. Woodchuck feels the season with skin that is so tight, he can't eat another bite. There's no denying that once again it is time to sleep.

Read aloud this book, and then reread it as a springboard for discussing the senses. In the mini-lesson that follows, children participate in a dramatic play activity that explores animals seeing, hearing, smelling, and feeling winter in the air.

Gather your students and their imaginations to sniff, slither, crawl, trudge, blink, burrow, perch, rumble, ramble, scritch-scratch, grumble, growl, curl-up, and snore like the animals in Denise Fleming's great book about animals preparing for a long winter's nap.

Mrs. L.: Every time I see the cover of *Time to Sleep* by Denise Fleming, I want to snuggle up beside Bear and take a nap.
Rebecca: I want to hug her.
Mrs. L.: What if you were a bear and I said, "It's time to sleep"?

Rich Vocabulary

rumbled *v.* made a loud sound like thunder

slithering *v.* crawling on the ground like a snake

Jared:	I'd growl at you.
Mrs. L.:	The bear in this story didn't. She "crawls into her cave and sleeps" –after she tells Snail that winter is coming. Do you remember how she knows it's time to sleep?
Jack:	She smells that it's time.
Mrs. L.:	Very good remembering. I'll reread that part: "Bear sniffed once. She sniffed twice. 'I smell winter in the air,' said Bear." Tell me what you think winter smells like.
Megan:	Cold.
Ben:	It smells like frost.
Michael:	I bet if you're a bear you know what winter smells like.
Mrs. L.:	I bet you're right. Bears have good sniffers and probably do know what winter smells like. See the leaf falling on the ground as Bear sniffs? I think winter smells like a pile of leaves that have fallen on the ground. Close your eyes, and pretend you're Bear. Sniff once. Sniff twice. Try to smell winter. I think I smell wood smoke in the air, too. What part of your body are you using to smell winter in the air?
Class:	Nose!
Mrs. L.:	Point to your nose. Great! You'll need your own space on the floor for this next part. Carefully crawl into your cave and sleep.
Ryan:	No! We have to tell Snail first.
Mrs. L.:	I'll look in the book to find out what Bear says to Snail. Here it is: "Snail was slowly slithering up one leaf and down another. 'Snail,' rumbled Bear, 'winter is in the air. It is time to seal your shell and sleep.'" Do you know how to rumble?
Rachel:	It's kind of a grumbly voice.
Mrs. L.:	Let's try it. Say, "Snail, winter is in the air" in a grumbly voice.
Class:	Snail, winter is in the air.
Mrs. L.:	Now rumble, "It is time to seal your shell and sleep."
Class:	It is time to seal your shell and sleep.
Mrs. L.:	How does Snail know winter is in the air?
Jack:	Bear told her.
Mrs. L.:	Yes, and she agrees with Bear because she has her own proof. I'll keep reading: "'You are right, Bear,' said Snail. 'This morning there was frost on the grass . . .'"
Jared:	She didn't smell it, she saw it.
Mrs. L.:	What part of her body did she use to see it?
Class:	Eyes!
Mrs. L.:	Point to your eyes. Good! Let's seal our shells and sleep, Snails.
Ryan:	No, we have to tell another animal first.
Mrs. L.:	Let's read to find out who she tells. "Snail was slithering on the leaves. She will slither to tell another animal." How do you slither?
Ben:	Slide like this. *(Ben slithers for the class.)*
Mrs. L.:	Great! Now who does Snail tell?
Class:	Skunk!
Mrs. L.:	Slither over to Skunk, and tell her the news.
Class:	Skunk, it's winter!

Mrs. L.: Nice job! Seal your shells and sleep. Goodnight, Snails.

Rachel: Now we're skunks!

Mrs. L.: Let's read what Skunk says when he hears the news from Snail: "Scritch, scratch. Scritch, scratch. Skunk was busy digging grubs. 'Skunk, winter is on its way,' said Snail. 'It is time for you to curl up in your den and sleep.'"

Blake: We skunks should be scritch, scratching in the dirt looking for bugs.

Jack: Grubs.

Mrs. L.: Right. Does Skunk believe Snail when she tells him it's time to sleep?

Ryan: Yes, because the leaves are red and yellow, and leaves change color when it's going to be winter.

Mrs. L.: What part of our bodies do we use to see the leaves changing colors?

Class: Our eyes.

Mrs. L.: Use your eyes to look up into the trees like Skunk did to see the leaves turning red and yellow.

Rebecca: Now we tell Turtle.

Mrs. L.: That's right. I'll read the next page: "Turtle was off on a ramble. 'Stop, Turtle!' cried Skunk. 'I have news. Winter is on its way.'"

Ryan: What's a ramble?

Zachary: Bear rambled—it was a growl.

Mrs. L.: That was a rumble. Turtle is rambling. It's a way of moving, like a slow walk.

Brittany: Turtles don't move very fast.

Mrs. L.: Pretend you're Skunk trying to catch up to Turtle to give him the news. Say, "Stop, Turtle! I have news."

Class: Stop, Turtle! I have news.

Mrs. L.: Winter is on its way.

Class: Winter is on its way.

Mrs. L.: Now Skunk can curl up in his den and sleep. Goodnight, skunks.

Jared: Read what Turtle says to skunk.

We continue reading, acting out, and discussing the remaining winter messengers' words. We discover that Woodchuck feels winter with tight skin. Ladybug sees winter in a sky full of geese. As Ladybug runs to find Bear to tell her it's time to crawl into her cave and sleep, she doesn't stop to notice Bear's already asleep in her cave. We end our lesson with a quick review of the five animals who know it's time to sleep.

It's Time to Sleep Senses Chart

Animal	Senses Winter How?	Where?	With?
Bear	smells winter	in the air	nose
Snail	sees winter	frost on the grass	eyes
Skunk	sees winter	red and yellow leaves	eyes
Turtle	sees winter	days growing shorter	eyes
Woodchuck	feels winter	tight skin	hands (body)
Ladybug	sees winter	sky full of geese	eyes

MORE FUN WITH THE BOOK

Animal puppets or stuffed animals can add an extra dimension of fun to the ending of a *Time to Sleep* lesson. Check your local library for bear, snail, skunk, turtle, woodchuck, and ladybug puppets, or put out a call to parents for puppets prior to this lesson. Just for fun, my students and I say goodnight using voices for each of the different animals via the puppets.

"Goodnight, Ladybug."

MANAGEMENT TIP

This chapter is filled with bedtime book-based activities to extend enjoyment and love of reading at home. If possible, have a few extra copies of the bedtime books in this chapter available to loan to children for at-home use. Place the books in individual Ziploc bags, and include a note card with directions. If paper and pencil are required for the activity, place these items in the bag as well. Following your book sharing time, draw a name from a hat for each bedtime book to be loaned. Invite children to bring in their own copies of the bedtime books shared to receive a book-based activity card to do at home.

You may wish to send home a monthly Bedtime Books Reading Log on which students and their parents record the books they've shared at bedtime. At the top of each new monthly log, highlight a title featured in this chapter, seasonal favorites, and student recommendations. Read the featured books for read-aloud early in the month to get children excited about sharing these books at home.

Think about offering small reading-related incentives to students for returning their logs at the end of each month. In addition to the warm and fuzzy time spent with a parent during book-sharing time, passing out stickers and/or bookmarks with favorite characters or allotting book-buddy time will reinforce the return of the reading logs.

Bedtime Books Reading Log

January

Record the favorite books you shared with your child at bedtime this month. If you read more than one book to your child at bedtime, please use this to highlight books shared rather than a means of listing *all* the books you've read.

Here are a few books to try this month.

Time to Sleep by Denise Fleming
Flora's Blanket by Debi Gliori
Owl Moon by Jane Yolen
The Snowy Day by Ezra Jack Keats
Oh My Baby, Little One by Kathi Appelt

Spotlight book: Megan R. recommends *Mr. Putter and Tabby Pour the Tea* by Cynthia Rylant because "Tabby looks like my cat!"

My Favorite Bedtime Books Read This Month

1	________	16	________
2	________	17	________
3	________	18	________
4	________	19	________
5	________	20	________
6	________	21	________
7	________	22	________
8	________	23	________
9	________	24	________
10	________	25	________
11	________	26	________
12	________	27	________
13	________	28	________
14	________	29	________
15	________	30	________

Parent Signature: ________ Student Signature ________

More Must-Have Bedtime Books

Goodnight Moon

by Margaret Wise Brown

Responding to Literature Through Writing

In the great green room
There was a telephone
And a red balloon
And a picture of—
The cow jumping over the moon …
— From *Goodnight Moon*, pages 2–4

> **Rich Vocabulary**
>
> **hush** *v.* to become quiet

Connect school to home with this classic published in 1947, which has been shared with generations of young children who take comfort in identifying their surroundings upon crawling into bed each night. Saying goodnight to special items brings closure to yet another day. And cuddling up with a loved one while reading a great book ends the day on a peaceful note.

At the end of the school day, read *Goodnight Moon,* and then conduct an impromptu survey asking who has a copy of the book at home. Pass out copies of the reproducible on page 93, which follows the pattern of the book. Children and parents are directed to look together for particular objects in their bedrooms and to make a connection with the book. Most of all, parents and children can enjoy a little good night, good book fun. Have a sharing time to allow students to highlight the discoveries they made when they said goodnight to things from something red to the moon.

TIPS FOR ENCOURAGING A LOVE OF READING AT HOME

- Have baskets or low shelves for books in every room, accessible to small children.
- Model reading with many different types of print.
- Set aside same time, same place reading—perhaps as a family activity.
- Talk about books read together, discuss favorite parts, illustrations, and other details.
- TURN OFF THE TV, and encourage other word-related pursuits.
- Visit the library on a regular basis and attend story times at local bookstores.

Pajama Time!

by Sandra Boynton

LEARNING
ABOUT

Responding to Literature Through Art and Writing

The moon is up.
It's getting late.
Let's get ready to celebrate.
It's Pajama Time!
— From *Pajama Time!*, page 2

After my preschoolers' rave reviews of *Blue Hat, Green Hat*, I decided to check out more Sandra Boynton books. When I shared *Pajama Time!* with my own children, they quickly ran upstairs to put on their favorite pair of "jammies" to pajama-dee-bop around the house. Whether they wear stripey, polka-dotted, fuzzy or not—kids will "pajammy" in whatever they've got.

Read aloud this rhyming book with a beat that will have students pajammying to the left, pajammying to the right, and wanting to share it at home that night! After children dance around in one big line and look so fine, tell them to hop to a quiet rest space and look at books independently.

After rest time, ask students to decorate a pair of paper pajama tops and bottoms to look like their favorites. Duplicate copies of the reproducible on page 94 for students to decorate with markers or crayons. They can also dictate or sound-spell a sentence to describe their pajamas.

It's Pajama Time!
My pajamas are

Rachel's pajamas are pink with stars.

MORE FUN WITH THE BOOK

Hold a Pajama Day as a reward for reading bedtime books at home. Send a note home to parents explaining that when the children have collectively read 100 bedtime books (or whatever number you deem appropriate), they will be invited to wear pajamas and slippers and to bring favorite bedtime stuffed animals to school. Display the monthly Bedtime Books Reading Logs (see page 82) on a Pajama Party Bulletin Board to keep track of the total number of books read.

> **Rich Vocabulary**
>
> **celebrate** *v.* to do something fun to remember a special time

Kiss Good Night

by Amy Hest

Strengthening Oral Language

Rich Vocabulary

arranged *v.* placed in a certain order

This is the tender story of a dark and stormy night on Plum Street as Mrs. Bear gets Sam ready for bed. After reading a book to him, tucking his blanket under his chin, arranging his friends around him just so, and joining him for a glass of milk, Mrs. Bear yawns. But Sam shakes his head and says he was waiting for something. After contemplating what she's forgotten in her routine of book, blanket, friends, and milk, at last she remembers—Sam's good night kiss. So book, blanket, friends, and milk become book, blanket, friends, milk, and kiss good night!

The bedtime ritual is comforting to Sam, who knows just what to expect when it comes to bedtime. The book-based activity in the box allows kids to put their bedtime routines into words. For extra oral language practice, repeat the pattern orally with a beat, as Mrs. Bear did with Sam: book, blanket, friends, milk, kiss good night.

Copy, cut out, and attach the box at right to a copy of *Kiss Good Night.*

Book-Based At-Home Fun with *Kiss Good Night*

In *Kiss Good Night*, Sam's bedtime routine is book, blanket, friends, milk, kiss good night. What is your bedtime routine? Write down 4 things you do every night to get ready for bed. Say the routine out loud with a beat. Don't forget a kiss good night!

Barnyard Lullaby

by Frank Asch

Identifying Sounds

As each new barnyard mother sings a beautiful lullaby to lull her babies to sleep, the farmer becomes increasingly agitated. The clock on the nightstand ticks from ten o'clock to nearly midnight as mothers hen, cow, pig, horse, sheep, and geese sing beautiful lullabies to their babies. To the farmer, it sounds like noisy clucking, neighing, mooing, oinking, baaing, and honking. Finally he yells, "Be quiet!" out the window, only to wake his own baby. "Now look what you've done!" mumbles his wife. As she sings a lullaby, her baby drifts off to sleep—and the farmer does, too.

After sharing this book for read-aloud, sing this lullaby to your students.

> *Gather round my children*
> *Sounds are buzzing in the air,*
> *Close your eyes and listen*
> *Then raise your hand to share.*

Rich Vocabulary

lullaby *n.* a song sung to help a baby go to sleep

Direct children to sit quietly and listen. After one minute or so, ask them to name a sound they heard during this quiet listening time. Although it may not be the honking of a goose, the neighing of a horse, or the baaing of a sheep, sounds such as the passing of a car, the roaring of a lawnmower, the ticking of a clock, the barking of a dog, or the chirping of a bird are everyday sounds that they might hear.

Next assign some quiet homework. Ask children to listen and remember sounds they hear at home when they're lying in bed. Then send *Barnyard Lullaby* home for some good book, good night fun.

Copy, cut out, and attach the box at right to a copy of *Barnyard Lullaby*.

Book-Based At-Home Fun with *Barnyard Lullaby* by Frank Asch

When the farmer in *Barnyard Lullaby* closed his eyes, he heard a lot of baaing, honking, clucking, mooing, and neighing.

1. Settle into bed, and read *Barnyard Lullaby.*
2. Close your eyes.
3. Listen to the nighttime sounds in your house for one minute.
4. Write down three sounds you hear.

Time for Bed

by Mem Fox

Reinforcing Listening Skills

Rich Vocabulary

gracious *adj.* good and kind

The phrase "time for bed" is dreaded by many an energized preschooler who's afraid of missing any fun and excitement by going to sleep. But in the context of this book, the words signal a time of loving, snuggling, and comfort with a loved one. As you read aloud this book, a warm-fuzzy feeling will envelope your classroom as the little sheep nuzzle nose to nose, mother cat and kitten snuggle in tight, the little fish makes a wish, and everyone realizes that "the whole wide world is going to sleep."

Following the read-aloud, sharpen students' listening skills by playing the Whisper a Secret game. Form a circle with children. Think of a secret to whisper into the ear of the student sitting on your left, such as "It's time for recess" or "It's time to go home." This student then whispers the secret to the student on his or her left. Play continues around the circle until the secret reaches the student sitting on your right. This student says the secret out loud. Compare your original secret and the final secret.

Then send a copy of this great book home with children to share with loved ones.

Copy, cut out, and attach the box at right to a copy of *Time for Bed.*

Book-Based At-Home Fun with *Time for Bed* by Mem Fox

Time for Bed Checklist

1. Snuggle into bed.
2. Read *Time for Bed*.
3. Turn out the light.
4. Check to see if the stars are out.
5. Name something that happened today that made you laugh.
6. Whisper a secret.
7. Make a wish.
8. Close your eyes.
9. Tell someone you love her or him.
10. Have one last kiss.

Sweet dreams, sleep well, good night!

How Do Dinosaurs Say Goodnight?

by Jane Yolen

Responding to Books Through Creative Play

How do dinosaurs say goodnight? Do they throw teddy bears, demand piggyback rides, or slam their tails and pout? Preschool children understand such expressions of anger and frustration—especially when there's the mention of something undesirable like saying good night. Share this book with your class to find out what really happens when the dinosaurs' mamas come in to say goodnight.

Jane Yolen's rhyming text and Mark Teague's comical illustrations make this book a great selection for preschool bookshelves. Who ever imagined a T-Rex snuggling with his blankie and holding his teddy bear as he heads off to bed, or a Triceratops sitting in a bathtub with a scrub brush?

After reading aloud this book, extend students' vocabulary by acting out some of the quieter actions of the dinosaurs. Together, identi-

Rich Vocabulary

pout *v.* to make a grumpy face because you're mad

fy what it means to mope, moan, sulk, pout, and sigh. Invite students to act out each action as a baby dinosaur would. Next try out the louder dinosaur behaviors—stomping feet, shouting, roaring, and perhaps some tail slamming.

Your students will be motivated to share this great dinosaur bedtime book at home. Together with a loved one, they can identify and search for each dinosaur's name hidden in the illustrations before saying good night.

Copy, cut out, and attach the box at right to a copy of *How Do Dinosaurs Say Goodnight?*.

Book-Based At-Home Fun with *How Do Dinosaurs Say Goodnight?* by Jane Yolen

1. Read *How Do Dinosaurs Say Goodnight?*
2. Reread the book, and look for the name of each dinosaur in each illustration. (*Tyrannosaurus Rex* is written on the bed's headboard. *Pteranodon* is written in blocks on the floor. *Trachodon* is on a wall banner, and so on.)
4. Extend vocabulary by acting out some of the "quieter" actions of the dinosaurs, for example, moping, moaning, sulking and sighing.
5. Reread the book upon request!

ON ANOTHER DAY

After another fun rereading, have children fill in missing text using rhyming word hints like the following:

> **Teacher:** Does a dinosaur stomp his feet on the floor and shout, "I want to hear"—
> **Children:** One book more!

Guess How Much I Love You

by Sam McBratney

Responding to Books Through Writing and Art

Little Nutbrown Hare, who was going to bed, held on tight to Big Nutbrown Hare's very long ears. He wanted to be sure that Big Nutbrown Hare was listening.

"Guess how much I love you," he said.

"Oh, I don't think I could guess that," said Big Nutbrown Hare.

"This much," said Little Nutbrown Hare, stretching out his arms as wide as they could go.

Big Nutbrown Hare had even longer arms. "But I love you this much," he said.

Hmm, that is a lot, thought Little Nutbrown Hare . . .

— From *Guess How Much I Love You*, pages 1–4

Thus begins the give-and-take of this tender bedtime book that proves love this big is hard to describe. Like Sam who refuses to go to sleep until his mother gives him a good-night kiss, Little Nutbrown Hare puts off going to bed until Big Nutbrown Hare guesses how much he loves him.

After sharing the book for read-aloud, encourage individual students to create a few new measures of love for the rest of the class to echo. Write the following sentences on the board or chart paper:

I love you as ________ as ________.

I love you all the way ________.

Here are some examples to get you started.

> *I love you as high as a skyscraper.*
> *I love you all the way to Grandma's house and back.*
> *I love you all the way up a rainbow.*

Rich Vocabulary

hare *n.* a rabbit

settled *v.* made calm

Record students' ideas on paper, and allow time for them to illustrate their ideas. Then send the book home with students. Like the other 49 books in this book, *Guess How Much I Love You* is a book for every family's bookshelf.

Copy, cut out, and attach the box below to a copy of *Guess How Much I Love You.*

Book-Based At-Home Fun with
***Guess How Much I Love You* by Sam McBratney**

After reading this book with your child, play the following oral language game to guess just how much you (Big Nutbrown Hare) and your child (Little Nutbrown Hare) love each other.

Big Nutbrown Hare: I love you this much. (Stretch arms wide.)

Little Nutbrown Hare: I love you this much. (Stretch arms wide.)

Big Nutbrown Hare: I love you as high as I can reach. (Reach high.)

Little Nutbrown Hare: I love you as high as I can reach. (Reach high.)

Big Nutbrown Hare: I love you all the way down to your toes. (Bend down.)

Little Nutbrown Hare: I love you all the way down to your toes. (Bend down.)

Big Nutbrown Hare: I love you as high as I can hop. (Hop in the air).

Little Nutbrown Hare: I love you as high as I can hop. (Hop in the air.)

Big Nutbrown Hare: I love you right up to the moon.

Little Nutbrown Hare: I love you right up to the moon—and back.

Tell Me Something Happy Before I Go to Sleep

by Joyce Dunbar

Strengthening Oral Language

"I can't sleep," said Willa.
"Why can't you sleep?" asked Willoughby.
"I'm afraid," said Willa.
"What are you afraid of?" asked Willoughby.
"I'm afraid that I might have a bad dream," said Willa.
"Think of something happy, then you won't have a bad dream," said Willoughby.

— From *Tell Me Something Happy Before I Go to Sleep*, page 5

Rich Vocabulary

longing *v.* wishing

When Willa can't think of something happy, her brother Willoughby gives her a few suggestions. As Willa falls asleep, she finally thinks of something happy—the happiest thing of all—having her brother there when she wakes up.

This delightfully cozy story of sibling revelry—not rivalry—makes a refreshing story to share for a preschool read-aloud. Discuss what a kind, thoughtful friend and brother Willoughby was by helping Willa think of happy things to fall asleep. Then make a list of Willa's happy things from the book, and brainstorm more happy things to display on a chart.

Attach the list of tell-me questions to a take-home copy of the book so parents can involve their children in a one-on-one book discussion of happy thoughts before they go to sleep.

Book-Based At-Home Fun with *Tell Me Something Happy Before I Go to Sleep* by Joyce Dunbar

Share these with your child.

- Tell me something happy.
- Tell me something that is the happiest thing of all.
- Tell me something you like waiting for you for breakfast.
- Tell me something waiting for you in your room.
- Tell me what you look forward to in the morning.
- Tell me someone you can't wait to see in the morning.
- Tell me your favorite toy.
- Tell me something that made you smile when you heard this book.
- Tell me what you like best about this book.

Flora's Blanket

by Debi Gliori

Strengthening Listening And Speaking Skills

As the mother of a small child who can't sleep without her blankie, I know how quickly a search party is called into action when it's bedtime and there's no blankie. I also know from experience that no substitute will suffice and that when the blankie is ultimately found, sleep comes nearly instantaneously to its owner.

When it's bedtime and Flora can't find her blanket, the whole family joins the search. As the bunnies search obvious and less obvious places, Flora begins to get sleepy. Will the family find her blanket so that they can all go to sleep?

Extend enjoyment of this bedtime tale by playing the following hide-and-seek game. Call on a volunteer to hide a blanket or another small object in a designated area while one child designated as Flora hides her eyes (no peeking!). As Flora searches for her lost blanket, the rest of the class gives hot and cold tips to help her adjust the search accordingly. If necessary, Flora can ask for help from a few of her siblings (fellow classmates). She can then "misplace" the blanket for the next child to find. Students will enjoy playing this game at home, as well.

Copy, cut out, and attach the box at right to a copy of *Flora's Blanket.*

Rich Vocabulary

offered *v.* tried to give something

odd *adj.* different

Book-Based At-Home Fun with *Flora's Blanket* by Debi Gliori

1. Read *Flora's Blanket.*
2. Have someone hide a "blanket" for you to find.
3. Pretend you're Flora trying to find your blanket.
4. Ask for hot and cold hints to help you find the blanket.
5. Hide the blanket for another family member to find.

Even More Must-Have Bedtime Books

"More More More," Said the Baby by Vera B. Williams
The Napping House by Audrey Wood
Lullaby Raft by Naomi Shihab Nye
The Sleepy Book by Charlotte Zolotow
The Big Red Barn by Margaret Wise Brown
So Many Bunnies: A Bedtime ABC and Counting Book by Rick Walton
Animal Crackers Bedtime by Jane Dyer
When Mama Comes Home Tonight by Eileen Spinelli
Sleepy Bears by Mem Fox
Counting Kisses by Karen Katz
Henry and Mudge and the Bedtime Thumps by Cynthia Rylant

Name ______________________________ Date ____________________

Good Night, Good Book Fun

I have the book, **Goodnight Moon,** at home. Yes ________ No ________

Parents: Read a copy of **Goodnight Moon** with your child. Together find objects from your child's bedroom to complete the sentences below that are patterned after the book. Send the completed page to school so your child can share some good night, good book fun.

In ____________________'s great ________________ room
(your child's name) (color)

There is a ________________

And a red ________________

And a picture of ________________

And there are 3 ________________

And 2 ________________

And a little toy ________________

And a(n) ________________

And a(n) ________________

And a(n) ________________

And a(n) ________________.

Goodnight room.

Goodnight moon.

Goodnight to everything in my room.

Use with *Goodnight Moon* by Margaret Wise Brown.

Name ______________________ Date ______________

It's Pajama Time!

Color the pajamas.

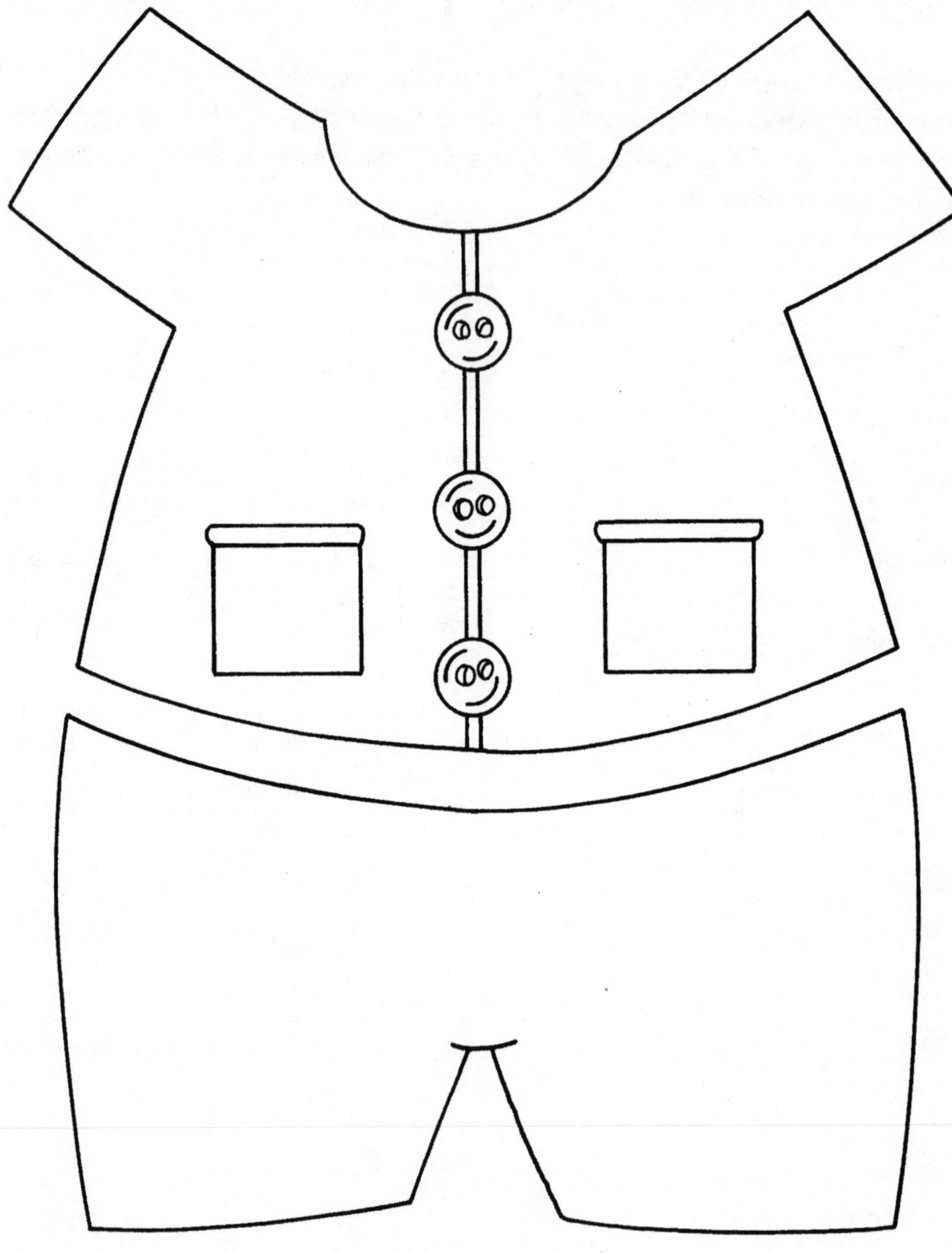

My pajamas are ______________________ .

Use with *Pajama Time!* by Sandra Boynton.

50 Must-Have Books for Preschool

Appelt, Kathi. *Oh My Baby, Little One*. New York: Harcourt, Inc., 2000.

Asch, Frank. *Barnyard Lullaby*. New York: Aladdin Paperbacks, 1998.

Baker, Alan. *White Rabbit's Color Book*. New York: Kingfisher Books, 1994.

Bang, Molly. *Ten, Nine, Eight*. New York: Greenwillow Books, 1983.

———. *When Sophie Gets Angry—Really, Really Angry*. New York: The Blue Sky Press, 1999.

Bond, Felicia. *Tumble Bumble*. New York: HarperTrophy, 1996.

Boynton, Sandra. *Blue Hat, Green Hat*. New York: Little Simon, 1984.

———. *Pajama Time!*. New York: Workman Publishing Company, 2000.

Brown, Margaret Wise. *Goodnight Moon*. New York: Harper & Row Publishers, Inc., 1947.

Carle, Eric. *1,2,3 to the Zoo: A Counting Book*. New York: The Putnam & Grosset Group, 1968.

———. *Hello, Red Fox*. New York: Simon & Schuster Books for Young Readers, 1998.

———. *The Mixed-Up Chameleon*. New York: Harper & Row, 1975.

———. *The Very Hungry Caterpillar*. New York: Philomel Books, 1969.

Curtis, Jamie Lee. *Today I Feel Silly and Other Moods That Make My Day*. New York: Scholastic, Inc., 1998.

Degan, Bruce. *Jamberry*. New York: HarperCollins Publishers, 1983.

dePaola, Tomie. *Tomie dePaola's Mother Goose*. New York: G.P. Putnam's Sons, 1985.

Dunbar, Joyce. *Tell Me Something Happy Before I Go to Sleep*. New York: Harcourt Brace & Company, 1998.

Ehlert, Lois. *Color Zoo*. New York: HarperCollins Publishers, 1989.

———. *Fish Eyes: A Book You Can Count On*. New York: Red Wagon Books, 1990.

———. *Planting a Rainbow*. New York: Harcourt Brace & Company, 1988.

Falconer, Ian. *Olivia*. New York: Scholastic, Inc., 2000.

Fleming, Denise. *Count!* New York: Henry Holt and Company, 1992.

———. *The Everything Book*. New York: Henry Holt and Company, 2000.

———. *Lunch*. New York: Henry Holt and Company, 1992.

———. *Time to Sleep*. New York: Henry Holt and Company, 1997.

Fox, Mem. *Time for Bed*. Orlando, FL: Harcourt Brace & Company, 1993.

Geisel, Theodore S. *Dr. Seuss's ABC*. New York: Random House, 1963.

———. *Mr. Brown Can Moo! Can You?* New York: Random House, 1970.

———. *My Many Colored Days*. New York: Alfred A. Knopf, 1996.

Gliori, Debi. *Flora's Blanket*. New York: Orchard Books, 2001.

Guarino, Deborah. *Is Your Mama a Llama?* New York: Scholastic, Inc., 1989.

Henkes, Kevin. *Wemberly Worried*. New York: Greenwillow Books, 2000.

Hest, Amy. *Kiss Good Night*. Cambridge, MA: Candlewick Press, 2001.

Hissey, Jane. *Little Bear's ABC and 123*. New York: Random House Children' Books, 2002.

Keats, Ezra Jack. *The Snowy Day*. New York: Penguin Books, 1962.

Kirk, David. *Miss Spider's ABC*. New York: Scholastic, Inc., 1998.

Lionni, Leo. *A Color of His Own*. New York: Alfred A. Knopf, 1975.

Martin, Bill, Jr. and Archambault, John. *Brown Bear, Brown Bear, What Do You See?* New York: Henry Holt and Company, 1967.

———. *Chicka Chicka Boom Boom*. New York: Simon & Schuster Books for Young Readers, 1989.

Mayo, Margaret. *Wiggle Waggle Fun*. New York: Alfred A. Knopf, 2000.

McBratney, Sam. *Guess How Much I Love You*. Cambridge, MA: Candlewick Press, 1994.

Opie, Iona, ed. *Here Comes Mother Goose*. Cambridge, MA: Candlewick Press, 1999.

———. *My Very First Mother Goose*. Cambridge, MA: Candlewick Press, 1996.

Prelutsky, Jack. *Read-Aloud Rhymes for the Very Young*. New York: Alfred A. Knopf, 1986.

Rankin, Laura. *The Handmade Alphabet*. New York: Dial Books for Young Readers, 1991.

Shaw, Nancy. *Sheep in a Jeep*. New York: Houghton Mifflin Company, 1986.

Steig, William. *Pete's a Pizza*. New York: HarperCollins Publishers, 1998.

Walsh, Ellen Stoll. *Mouse Paint*. New York: Harcourt Brace & Company, 1989.

Wells, Rosemary. *Morris's Disappearing Bag*. New York: Puffin Books, 1999.

Yolen, Jane. *How Do Dinosaurs Say Goodnight?* New York: The Blue Sky Press, 2000.

Preschool Learning Skills

READING AND WRITING

Reading fluency

My Very First Mother Goose, pp. 8–11

Exploring the beat of rhyming language

Wiggle Waggle Fun, pp. 14–15
Tumble Bumble, pp. 17–18

Exploring sounds

Barnyard Lullaby, pp. 85–86
Mr. Brown Can Moo! Can You?, pp. 18–19

How print is organized

Tomie dePaola's Mother Goose, pp. 15–16

Letter and sound recognition

Chicka Chicka Boom Boom, pp. 46–47
Dr. Seuss's ABC, pp. 49–50
Jamberry, pp. 20–21
Little Bears ABC and 123, pp. 43–45

Letter-sound relationships

Dr. Seuss's ABC, pp. 49–50
The Handmade Alphabet, pp. 47–48

Listening and speaking skills

Flora's Blanket, p. 91
Is Your Mama a Llama?, pp. 19–20
Kiss Good Night, p. 85
Morris's Disappearing Bag, p. 33
Olivia, pp. 31–32
Read-Aloud Rhymes for the Very Young, pp. 13–14
Tell Me Something Happy Before I Go to Sleep, p. 90
Time for Bed, pp. 86–87

Responding to literature

Through creative play and art:
Guess How Much I Love You, pp. 88–89
How Do Dinosaurs Say Goodnight?, pp. 87–88
Pajama Time!, p. 84
Through writing:
Goodnight Moon, p. 83
Guess How Much I Love You, pp. 88–89
Pajama Time!, p. 84

Vocabulary awareness

Color words:
Blue Hat, Green Hat, p. 74
Color Zoo, p. 72
Identifying the senses:
Time to Sleep, pp. 79–82
Rhyming words:
Here Comes Mother Goose, pp. 12–13
Sheep in a Jeep, pp. 16–17

Writing

Printing letters:
Miss Spider's ABC, pp. 48–49
Goodnight Moon, p. 83
Pajama Time, p. 84

MATH

Counting:
Count!, pp. 54–55
The Everything Book, pp. 34–35
Fish Eyes, pp. 50–51
Graphing:
The Everything Book, pp. 34–35
Lunch, p. 66
Numbers:
Count!, pp. 54–55
Ten, Nine, Eight, p. 54
The Very Hungry Caterpillar, p. 52
One-to-one correspondence:
Fish Eyes, pp. 50–51
1,2,3 to the Zoo, pp. 55–56
Shapes:
Color Zoo, p. 72
The Everything Book, pp. 34–35
Sorting by color:
Planting a Rainbow, p. 73

ART (COLORS)

Color patterns:
The Mixed-Up Chameleon, pp. 69–70
Color words:
Blue Hat, Green Hat, p. 74
Color Zoo, p. 72
Complementary colors:
Hello, Red Fox, pp. 68–69
Graphing colors:
The Everything Book, pp. 34–35
Lunch, p. 66
Recognizing colors:
Brown Bear, Brown Bear, What Do You See?, p. 67
A Color of His Own, p. 71
Lunch, p. 66
Mouse Paint, pp. 62–64
White Rabbit's Color Book, p. 70
Sorting by color:
Planting a Rainbow, p. 73

PERSONAL GROWTH

Emotions and Feelings

Adjusting feelings:
Pete's a Pizza, p. 38
Anger:
When Sophie Gets Angry—Really, Really Angry…, pp. 26–29
Depicting emotions:
The Everything Book, pp. 34–35
The Snowy Day, pp. 36–37
Expressing emotions:
My Many Colored Days, pp. 35–36
Oh My Baby, Little One, p. 37
Identifying feelings:
Today I Feel Silly and Other Moods That Make My Day, pp. 30–31
Relating to a character's feelings:
Wemberly Worried, pp. 32–33